TWICE IN A LIFETIME

Deborah E. Comeaux

Copyright © [2023] by [Deborah E. Comeaux]

All rights reserved.

No portion of this book may be reproduced in any form without written permission from the publisher or author, except as permitted by U.S. copyright law.

Dedication

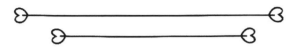

This book is dedicated to my daughters Shawn and Charlotte, my granddaughters Davian, Caelan, BraeLynn & Sydney. I am so grateful to each of you for your love, support and inspiration. You are God gifts to me. I love you each more than you know.

Table of Contents

Acknowledgements: 1

My First Love 3

My Shattered World 16

Preparing For The Final Goodbye 19

Trying To Move Past The Pain 37

Learning It's Okay To be Love & Love Again 40

Our Wedding Day 54

Move Preparation 37

Disobedience and Church Drama 46

Wolves In Sheep's Clothing 48

The Cult's Deceptive Plan (some quotes taken from psychology today magazine) 97

Spiritual Captivity 57

Purpose & Identity 59

False Teachers/False Prophets 106

God Restored Our Marriage & Our Family 62

Saying Goodbye To A Significant Part of Our Lives
.... 76

After The Loss 79

The Funeral & Final Goodbyes 143

Helpful Tips 87

Life After 88

Nothing before Its Time By Clarence L. Haynes Jr.
.... 177

The Broken-hearted Widow 180

Acknowledgements

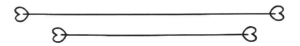

I would like to thank my high school friend Francis House, who God reconnected me to in 2018. Thank you for our therapy heart to heart talks, laughter and prayer time. It's been a blessing to share with someone who understands the loss of a spouse and living with chronic pain daily.

I will never forget the nurture, compassion & love of my mom who died when I was 14 years old. My older sisters: **Laura** who offered wisdom and support as she searched for truth and comfort in God's word while suffering with chronic joint pain from rheumatoid arthritis. **Anna** who guided and protected me after mom died. My sisters **Evelyn, Judy and Ella** were excellent cooks. I learned a lot from each of my sisters. **Judy** had a gift of hospitality. I always felt so welcome and comfortable in her home. **Ella** was my Wednesday prayer partner, we prayed for every family member by name for years until her health took a drastic change. My youngest brother, **Kenneth**, is compassionate and a giver. He has also been a voice of reason for me many times. Remembering the times **Carl** offered his apartment to Charles and I when we lived in California. He had a nice place on the beach and when he went away for the weekend, he would let us know that his place was available if we needed to get away. These were some very special times for us, since we always loved being on the beach or near it. **Jimmy** especially played a special role in my life when I went to California as a teenager and when Drew (my first husband) and I living in California. We had some fun times with Jimmy. **Lernest, (my** eldest brother) even though we're approximately 17 years apart, Charles and I had some special times filled with laughter with Lernest and his wife **Laura**. It was so special to have my siblings; **Lernest, Ella, Nolan, Carl &**

Kenneth for support as I went through my grieving process as a widow. They were all there for me in in a special way. We shared some special times together that will always be dear to me. There's always prayer and a lot of laughter when we were together. God has done a great work in my family over the years. I miss my brother Nolan who transitioned in 2019.

My First Love

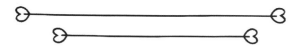

Drew & I lived near each other, there was a main cross street that separated our neighborhoods. He was friends with one of my brothers. Later, we became friends, and I would help him babysit his cousins who were toddlers and so adorable. Everyone that knew me, knew that I loved children. Babysitting was my very first job. I always thought Drew was handsome but did not think he would ever be interested in me in that way. Besides, he had a choice of several beautiful girls that were after him in school. I did not want to just be a number or another girl in his black book, I desired a more meaningful & lasting relationship, and I wasn't settling for less.

We had great conversations and a lot of laughter when we spent time together. He was compassionate, generous, and always willing to help the downtrodden. When my mom died in January 1970, I was 14 years old, Drew was there to comfort and listen to me. He knew how I felt about my mom. My mom made everyone feel special when they came to our house; in return, she was loved by all our friends. Shortly after her death, he told me he had joined the Marines and would be leaving soon for boot camp. By this time, I was in love with him. I was heartbroken that he was leaving. Meanwhile, we enjoyed each other's company until that time. It was comforting & fun to have all my sisters together. There were six girls and five boys at the time of mom's death. We heard we had a younger brother that died at toddler age, which was 12 children in all. When it was time for the California siblings to leave it was sad, and the house felt empty.

I felt so much anger toward my dad. I didn't tell any of my siblings until we were all adults. I lost respect for my dad and became so rebellious toward him. He would tell me to be home at a certain time and I would come in an hour later. Ella would be so afraid for me because I was disciplined for disobeying. She said, girl what is wrong with you, do you like getting in trouble? I didn't care at the time and didn't know what to do with this secret information. sometimes I could hear my mom crying. After my mom died, my dad continued seeing this woman. He came to pick me and my brothers up from Laura's house after he and Ms Rita came from a bingo game. I wanted to stay with my sisters, and he said you have to cook breakfast for your brothers in the morning. Once I got in the car, he said, say hello to Ms. Rita.

I refused and called her out of her name. I was so bitter after my mom died. My younger brother followed my bad example and did the same thing.

My middle brother said hello trying to be respectful as we were brought up. Dad said once he dropped Ms Rita home, he would be back to discipline us. My younger brothers sat on my bed until daddy came home, we all got in trouble because of my attitude and disobedience. I didn't like the woman and I just didn't want to be forced to be around her especially days after my mom's death and knowing that my dad was with her before my mom's death was still an open wound to me. My younger brothers didn't know about this at the time. I kept it to myself for years. After a couple of years went by, I eventually accepted that my dad was going to be with her and there was nothing I could do about it. She invited me over to eat one day once Drew and were married. I went to visit my dad and she made a homemade vegetable beef soup; it was delicious but a little spicy for me. My dad loved spicy foods.

During the 70s most of my female classmates had an autograph book and we chose special friends to share something inspiring or encouraging in it. **Drew wrote-** I will miss you! I have heard that absence makes the heart grow fonder. I was hoping this would be true in our case. When it was time for him to leave, I rode with his mom to the airport. We hugged and I cried like a baby. My favorite song at that time was "Love on a Two-Way Street." Every time I heard that song, I thought of Drew and cried. He called to let me, and his mom knew that he made it safe to Memphis for bootcamp. He asked me to check on his mom as often as possible. When he could not reach her, he was concerned, He would ask me to go to his house and see if she was home. I did not find out until later that she had attempted suicide more than once when Drew and his brother Jude were younger. Loretta was a beautiful woman whom I thought had nothing to be sad or depressed about. As I have learned, outward appearance does not mean that everything is great on the inside. I should know, I practiced it well. I would dress fashionably like a model but the void and pain I was experiencing on the inside did not match with the outside. Andrew, her husband, was in the navy and had been for several years because he kept re-enlisting.

The family traveled with him when the boys were young, but Loretta was close to her parents and wanted to remain in Louisiana near them. Andrew (Drew's dad) was in the Navy for 20 plus years. Loretta eventually started seeing someone else and was with him for several years. I am not sure if the separation was legal or if his parents were divorced. Drew and his brother Jude learned to accept and love this man because he loved their mother.

I lost touch with Loretta and Drew once I moved to California in November 1970. My dad decided it was best for me to go live with my older sisters in California. I was acting out to get attention from my dad, it did not matter if it was negative attention, I just wanted to feel loved and accepted by my dad. He told me I was responsible for taking care of my two younger brothers who were 9 & 12 years old. I resented him for putting that pressure on me. I was so devastated over the loss of my mother and so were my younger brothers. We had no adult supervision; we were free to come and go as we pleased. When there was no food in the house, we would put on our Sunday best to go to the church where there was always a wedding or a funeral on Saturdays and plenty of food. We learned how to survive quickly.

Living in California as a teenager was quite an experience for a country girl. My cousin asked me where I wanted to go, and I said Hollywood. I was looking out the car window waiting for the glamour and lights, I said, how long will it be before we get to Hollywood? He said, we are in Hollywood! I was shocked, it was nothing like I imagined. That hurt broken young girl was still crying on the inside, putting on a facade because there was no safe place to share what I was going through. On a positive note, my sisters Evelyn and Judy did their best to make life fun for me, we spent a lot of time together and laughed a lot as usual in my family.

In February 1971, my sister Anna moved to San Fernando Valley from Lake Charles, Louisiana to live with my cousin and his family. On February 9, 1971, San Fernando had an earthquake with a magnitude of 6.5 to 6.6. It affected the Greater Los Angeles area and Southern California.

I was living in Compton, California at the time. This was my first earthquake experience, and it was terrifying! We were all concerned about Anna and our family in San Fernando. It was several hours before we heard from Anna. Within a few days, Anna called to let us know she would see us in a couple of days. I was so glad to see her, I was closer to her because she was living in Louisiana with me when our mother was dying. Ella, Anna & I stayed at the hospital with mom during her last days. Anna understood what I was going through, and it was a comfort having her near me. I eventually moved in with Anna and her husband.

My brother Jimmy spent a lot of time with me. He would take me to his basketball games, we would go out for pizza and conversations. He also allowed me to clean his nice bachelor's apartment and he would pay me so I would have some spending money. Plus, just having a place to be by myself and listening to some good music was a nice experience. He was a good big brother with a kind heart.

My sisters saw that I was homesick and how much I missed my sisters (Ella & Laura) in Louisiana, so they surprised me with a ticket to go back home. I was so thankful and glad to get home to see Ella & my new niece Dwana who was around 4 months at the time. Ella was staying with my oldest sister Laura, and I decided that's where I wanted to be and I wouldn't go back to the family house, it was falling apart and very depressing for me since I saw that life could be better just being with my sisters.

Laura was diagnosed with Rheumatoid Arthritis shortly after she was married. She was able to work until her early 20s. I remember her wearing special shoes for support and she kept getting worse and started using crutches. As her health continued to decline, the rest of her days was from bed to wheelchair and vice versus. She had two stillbirth pregnancies and one living daughter that she had custody of after her divorce. After she lost her son, momma insisted she stay with us so she could get all the help she needed to recover. She needed help with eating, walking and bathing. My mom made sure Laura and Maggie were cared for when she was alive. Maggie was with us most of the time. She was more like a sister to us than a niece.

I could see where Laura felt left out at times because of her limitations. I admired her so much and trusted her advice. She was wise beyond her years and had learned a thing or two from her life experiences. I remembered Laura would watch Oral Roberts, Billy Graham & Jimmy Swaggart regularly.

In September 1971, Laura called out to me to tell me that on the local news they reported, Loretta Guillory (Drew's mom died of a self-inflicted gunshot wound to the head/temple). I could not believe what I was hearing! I watched the evening news with Laura just to be sure that this was true. It was confirmed on the evening news. I felt so sad for Drew & Jude, but I was looking forward to seeing Drew again.

Within a few days, I heard a knock on the door and opened it. I smiled when I saw Drew standing there. He said I'm so glad you answered the door & hugged me tightly. He said he went to the old family house, but no one was there. I invited him in, and he said hello to everyone. He asked me if I would go out to dinner with him. I checked with Laura to make sure it was okay. Drew needed to talk, and I wanted to be there for him like he was for me when my mom died. After that night, I don't remember a day that we were apart while he was on leave. The next time we went out for dinner, he asked if it was ok for Jude to come with us because he did not want to leave him alone.

Loretta planned her suicide; she insisted that Jude go spend the weekend with his cousins. Jude said he sensed something was wrong, he did not want to go but Loretta convinced him to go. Drew decided to ask for extended leave because of the trauma that he and his family were dealing with.

Andrew (his dad) came back home from the Navy after Loretta's death and eventually remarried. Drew had some resentment towards his dad, but I convinced him to give his dad another chance, which he did. We started going to dad's house regularly.

In October 1971, Drew asked me to marry him, I was shocked that he was ready for this kind of commitment. His experience in joining the Marines helped him to grow up. My dad had back surgery and was bedridden for 3 months. He lived with my aunt Edith at the time. She cared for him as she did with many others.

Drew asked my dad for my hand in marriage, my dad was like, yes! I was 15 and Drew was 18. He wanted to marry me before he went back to Camp Pendleton California. We knew that since I was a minor my dad would have to be there to give his approval by signing a document. Since he could not, we asked Laura if she would sign for me. Not checking with the Orange, Texas courthouse before going there was a big mistake. It was Laura, Elton (Drew's cousin), Rose (his aunt), and Drew in the car.

It was 36 miles from Lake Charles. We were all dressed up and excited. Elton & Drew carried

Laura in her wheelchair up several steps in front of the courthouse to get inside and find out that Laura had to be my legal guardian, or my had to be deceased for her to sign for me. We were so disappointed and sorry we did not check into this beforehand. Laura was so excited about being a part of the wedding. She had this cough that sometimes once she started was constant for a while.

On the way home, Aunt Rose asked if she was okay and she said she was, but Drew and I were concerned. Once we got Laura home, we made sure she ate, was comfortable, and made sure she took her meds. Her cough subsided some.

On October 10, 1971- Drew and I were at his Aunt Rose's place in the country riding bikes. When we went back to the house, there was an emergency message for me to call my brother Nolan. I called him at Laura's house, and he said, Laura died. I paused for a minute to make sure I was hearing right. Nolan said that the persistent cough started, and she choked. Drew & I headed to Laura's house to be with family. Laura's daughter Maggie was 10 years old; later she moved with her dad to Houston after her mom's death.

It was now time for Drew to head back to Camp Pendleton, it was hard to let him go, but I knew he would be back the following year so that we could get married. My dad would be able to be at the courthouse this time.

On December 2, 1972- I married my first love, I was 16 years old, and he was 19 years old. He was a first-class private marine at the time and still stationed in California. We decided to get married at the courthouse in Beaumont Texas. We had a small reception at my sister & brother in law's house. Drew started doing some carpentry work for a neighbor who had some rental properties. The lady loved the work he did and asked him if he would work for her. She told him that we could move into the one-bedroom house since it was freshly painted and remodeled. The house had a nice big yard.

About a month after we were married, I started having morning sickness and decided to set an appointment with an OB/GYN. The doctor said I was about three weeks pregnant with a possible due date of September 29[th.] We both were so excited about the pregnancy. Drew was overprotective and watched my every move. When Drew first enlisted in the Marines it was partially to make his mom proud. Once she passed, that desire was not there. He was a hard worker and always was ready to learn new things.

Since things were looking up for us, he decided he did not want to go back, he was enjoying civilian life too much. I tried to convince him to go back, and then we would be free to live our lives in peace. Nothing I said changed his mind. My brother-in-law got him on at the same company he was working for.

I received a call from Drew one day letting me know that he was calling from downtown jail. The U.S. Marshall had issued a warrant for his arrest for being AWOL, and he was arrested on the job. They allowed me to visit him before his flight out to California the next day. He was sentenced to serve 4 months in the brig.

The plan was once he completed serving his time, he would start the search for a nice apartment in a city near the base, neither of us wanted to live on base. Drew found a nice apartment in Santa Ana, California. The doctor gave me the okay to travel at 6 1/2 months pregnant. The morning sickness (hyperemesis gravidarum) was severe, on the plane, I was sick and kept running to the bathroom.

I ended up missing my layover in Orange County Airport. Next thing I knew I was in San Francisco, California which was approximately 414 miles from Santa Ana. I was wearing a summer short sleeve sun dress. It was so cold in San

Francisco. My jacket was in a larger suitcase. The airline clerk said that I would have to buy another ticket to fly to Los Angeles and then pay for a ticket to fly back to Orange County Airport from there. I was so sick, cold, and tired from the long trip.

There were no cell phones back then, so I called Drew from a payphone from the airport in San Francisco to let him know what was going on. He was worried and had called my family in Texas to make sure I left on time. Once I arrived in Los Angeles, I bought a ticket for the next plane out to Orange County airport. From Orange County, I took a cab to our apartment. Drew was anxiously waiting outside for me.

He paid the cab driver and grabbed my luggage. We called my family in Los Angeles and in Texas to let them know I made it home safe. Drew had a hot bubble bath waiting for me and he prepared dinner. The place was clean, I told him how proud I was of him for finding a nice apartment in such a quiet and beautiful neighborhood. The only thing was that we would have to move before the baby was born. No children were allowed, we tried to convince the manager of the apartment complex to let us stay after the baby was born. She said if she did that for us and others will expect the same. While we lived there, we enjoyed the nice neighborhood and did a lot of walking.

We had family over often. My brother Jimmie & his girlfriend would come to visit, and we would go for rides or a hike in Griffith Park in Los Angeles. Yes, I hiked while I was pregnant. Of course, I was 17 years old then and California's weather was so beautiful. I was always on the go once the worst part of morning sickness passed. I still experienced it throughout my nine months, it just wasn't like the earlier months when it was most of the day.

We ended up moving closer to my family to have someone nearby just in case Drew was working when I went into labor. On the morning of August 23, 1973, I noticed that my water bag was leaking and called my doctor. He told me to go to the hospital and he would meet me there. Once the doctor examined me, he said I had only dilated 2 centimeters. Drew came straight to the hospital after he got off from work. I sent him home to rest since the doctor informed us that the baby and I would be monitored for a few hours, and nothing would be happening anytime soon. Our daughter was born on August 24, 1973, at 4:36 am after several long hours of labor. I chose her first name, and he chose her middle name (Lucretia Roshawn).

Living in California was difficult financially. Drew worked 8:00-5:00 on base and from 6:00 pm to 10:00 pm at a department store and later took a third job for a brief period. I convinced him to allow me to get a job also. I was excited and started working at Winchell Donuts. Within a week of working, I received a call from the babysitter saying

Shawn had a fever and was vomiting. The only babysitters I used were my sister Judy for a date night, her mother-in-law or my sister Evelyn's friend. When I had doctor appointments at the hospital there was a daycare for mothers to use. When Drew and I would go visit my sister Evelyn, her daughter loved pushing Shawn in the stroller with her friends next door. I had to keep an eye on them, so they wouldn't forget that she wasn't a baby doll.

After several calls about Shawn being sick and trying to keep a job, Drew & I decided it was best for me to stay home with Shawn. Drew was under so much stress. I wanted to help and give him some relief. There was a time when Drew mentioned to me after the incident that he had chest pains, and I convinced him to set an appointment. The doctor on base told him it was growing pains, and nothing was wrong with his heart.

Drew was upset and wouldn't agree to another appointment for a second opinion. He didn't have faith in military doctors. We made the best of our weekends by spending time with family. Most of the time we were at Judy & Charles house since they had a pool. Then there were other times we hung out with Jimmy & his girlfriend.

My sister Ella came to visit with her father-in-law & his wife. Shawn was about 10 months old, and Ella was so glad to spend time with her since she wasn't able to be there for her birth. She asked when we were going to visit Beaumont, Texas? I told her I was not sure because it was not financially possible at the time. Ella suggested that we let Shawn go home with her and maybe I could work and raise the money to go pick up Shawn, she concluded, and this will give you a chance to visit too.

Drew totally left the decision up to me about letting Ella take Shawn. He did not want any part of it because he knew me too well. He did not want to be the blame when I started to miss my baby. He was so right! I cried a lot missing her so much. When I talked to her on the phone, she was excited to hear my voice and talked to me in her baby language. I was convinced that she missed me as much as I missed her.

We raised the money and purchased me a ticket to go to Beaumont to be with my baby in Beaumont, Texas. By this time Drew's term was almost over and he would be discharged from the marines. We decided that it would be best for me to stay there, and he would join me then. Meanwhile, I found a job in Beaumont and Drew chose for me to receive a monthly allotment. When Drew arrived months later, we stayed with Ella & Ed until Drew found a job. Shortly after, we found an apartment close by.

Drew found a full-time job and did carpentry work to make extra money. Our money went further in Texas than in California. The cost of living was so affordable. We both were glad to be home and we could now visit our dads in Lake Charles, LA.

My Shattered World

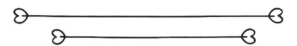

On June 25, 1975, Drew came home from work and did what he usually did, which was to spend time with Shawn. He would take her for a walk and visit his aunt who lived close by.

I prepared one of his favorite meals, garfish cooked in tomato sauce. He came home exhausted, but he knew we were expecting company that evening so he took a bath. I fed Shawn, bathed her and put her to bed early. Drew's cousin Carrie & her husband Walter arrived shortly after. We laughed, talked, and listened to music. I could still hear the O'Jays song "Stairway to Heaven" playing in my head for many months after that night. I noticed that Drew seemed restless, He walked from the living room to the kitchen back & forth. I excused myself to go check on him and asked if he was ok. He said that his chest felt like something heavy was pressing on it. I thought he was tired and needed rest.

I explained to Carrie & Walter that Drew was not feeling well, and he was going to bed. After they left, I went to the bedroom to check on Drew, he was still restless. He jumped up and took his shirt off and went to the living room where the window air condition unit was, and he stood right in front of it. I called out to him saying, baby, you should not stand so close to the a/c. I wrapped my arms around him to walk him back to the bedroom. We never made it to the bedroom; he collapsed by the bathroom door. I called out his name, but he did not answer, then I noticed the frothing at the mouth, which I later learned was terminal respiratory secretions known as the death rattle. I did not know what was happening to him, but I knew this was profoundly serious. We did not have a landline phone, so I grabbed Shawn & ran next door to our landlord's house and told her what happened and asked her if I could use her phone to call the paramedics. I also called Carrie & Walter to let them know what was going on. They assured me that they would be there shortly. She grabbed my hand and said the Lord's prayer.

  Her granddaughter kept Shawn while I went back to my apartment to wait for the paramedics. 45 minutes went by and there were still no paramedics, and they were located 2 blocks from where we lived. By this time, neighbors were in the driveway curiously looking. Walter and Carrie arrived; Walter went straight to check on Drew. He stuck his hand in Drew's mouth and grabbed his tongue, for a few minutes Drew came back and started having flashbacks from his time overseas in war, the paramedics were finally in the driveway. They put him on the stretcher, gave him oxygen and I got in the ambulance with him.

He looked over at me and said, hey baby! I was so glad to hear his voice. Before we made it to the hospital, He was pronounced dead (DOA). The ER doctors tried to resuscitate him, and this gave me some hope that he would come back like he did the first time. Maybe the doctors and medical team will revive him again. A few minutes later, the doctor came out to tell us that they could not save him.

I could not believe what I was hearing. Some of my family members were with me, but I felt so alone. My heart ached so bad; I was waiting to wake up from this horrible nightmare. The next day, I realized that it was real, Drew would no longer come in from work to greet me or pick up his baby for them to go on their daily walk. Each day my heart ached even more than the day before. I cried day and night and became so depressed, wondering how I could stop this pain in my heart. There was no pill that I could take to relieve the pain. The days were long and the nights seemed never ending.

Preparing For The Final Goodbye

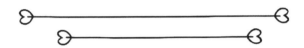

My father-in-law and brother-in-law came in from Louisiana for us to go to the funeral home to view the body before the memorial service. When I walked into the living room and saw their faces, I burst into tears because they looked so much like Drew. My legs were like limp noodles, I was going down when my father-in-law reached out to hold me up. I said I cannot do this; I just want to die!

He said, Deborah, you must be strong for Shawn, she needs you now! I had the strength to make it through that day because of his encouragement and his reminding me of what was important. I was in & out with waves of grief and depression.

My heart ached so bad. My sister Ella and my friend Linda helped me with Shawn when some days I just cried for hours and did not want her to see me like that. I had never experienced pain like this before, even though I lost my mother when I was 14 years old, a sister the year after mom, and my mom's sister (my aunt) who was like a grandmother to me.

This pain seemed so unbearable, and no one understood what I was going through. I already had put up walls from my childhood experiences of molestation, rejection & loss. More walls are going up now to protect my heart from pain and more trust issues.

I said it is just going to be Shawn & me from now on. Family and friends said, you are still young, you will meet someone and fall in love again. I did not want to hear that because, in my young mind, my plan was to be married to one man for my lifetime.

1 Timothy 5:14 (NIV)

So, I advise these younger widows to marry again, have children, and take care of their own homes. Then the enemy will not be able to say anything against them.

At one point in life, it was hard to believe that anyone could love me for who I was. I always thought once they got to know me that they would leave me. Here was this kind-hearted, handsome man, who loved me dearly & now he was gone.

While still attending the catholic church, I started going for counseling sessions with the priest. I left there feeling so empty and uncomforted. Maybe because he didn't really understand what I was going through. Thank God for my friend Linda at the time she would just listen to me when I needed to talk. She allowed me to express myself even though she did not understand the pain I felt. I continued putting one foot in front of the other each day for Shawn.

Shawn came to me one day and hugged me tight, she said, momma, everything is gonna be ok. I burst into tears and thought, wow, my 2-year-old daughter could see I was hurting. She tried to comfort me when I should have been the one reassuring her that everything was going to be ok. Of course, she could not understand why she was not seeing her dad anymore. The dad who came home from work and immediately prepared for their daily walk to his Aunt Josephine's house.

Trying To Move Past The Pain

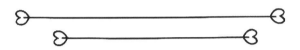

In that same year, while still grieving Drew's death and dealing with depression most days. I asked my sister if I could work at least one day a week, just to get out of the house. She worked at my aunt & uncle's grocery/liquor store. While I was working there, one day this handsome man came in, our eyes locked while we checked it other out. He said you are so pretty! He introduced himself and I told him my name. He asked if I was married, and I told him that my husband passed. He apologized for being so forward. He gave his condolences and said he would see me again since this was a regular stop for him after work. Well, I did not see him for a while since I did not work every day. About a month later, he came in on a day that I had my daughter with me. He spoke to her and commented on how pretty she was, she was shy and hid behind me. He asked me out on a date, I was excited but hesitant.

Once I told my sister, she and a friend encouraged me to go. They helped me pick out an outfit. I almost canceled; my emotions were all over the place. I was feeling guilty about going out on a date so soon. Once we arrived at the restaurant, we continued our conversations from our ride there. He told me he had been separated from his first wife for a couple of years and there were no plans of reconciliation. He was living with his dad at the time. I felt comfortable being with him and talking to him, and he was a good listener. I waited several months before I allowed Shawn to be around Charles. I wasn't sure where our relationship was going and if it would last. We took her on one of our rides to the country, she sat in between us since there were no seatbelt laws at the time. Charles brought her some cheetos and juice, she was happy. At one point she looked over at Charles and said daddy? I couldn't hold the tears back. I said no baby, that's not daddy. After that day, there were a lot of outings including Shawn. While I was waiting for insurance money and other income to come through, things were tight financially. When Charles offered financial help, I refused. He told Ella to talk to me and help me realize that we all need help at times. I was living with my friend Linda and my cousin Linda at the time. They allowed me to rent the third bedroom after their previous roommate moved out. Charles surprised Shawn with a cake, balloons and gifts for her second birthday. To see the excitement on that cute little face brought me so much joy! He did things like that often for me and Shawn. People that didn't know me and Drew's story assumed that Shawn was Charles's daughter since they both had green eyes.

Learning It's Okay To be Love & Love Again

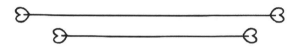

On date nights with Charles, after dinner, we would sit on the hood of his car (Electra 225 Buick) the car street name was called, "deuce and a quarter". We would watch the beautiful stars & evening moonlight. I was not able to see the beauty of God's creation since I was blinded with grief until Charles started pointing out the beauty of the stars, sky, birds, and flowers. I slowly started smiling and laughing again. There were days I just wanted to be alone or hang out with Linda. We would walk to the park behind St. Anne's church and stop at Dairy Queen afterwards. Those simple things were fun and refreshing. Shawn was with us sometimes and other times she stayed with Ella. Linda and Ella helped me a lot with Shawn, especially on those days where I was depressed and couldn't stop crying, I didn't want her to see me like that.

On those cloudy days I thought of my aunt (my mom's sister) and wondered how she made it through after losing her husband. They were so close; it was only them, no children. I remember her crying uncontrollably on the day of the funeral. I observed and saw her in pain and didn't know what to do, I was in elementary school then. I loved her and her husband. They were like grandparents to us. They were compassionate people. She and my mom were very close, and she was protective over my mom.

Even though I was in a relationship with Charles. I would still cry when I thought about Drew. Of course, when I looked at Shawn and saw Drew in that little face and thought she would never know him and how much he loved her, it broke my heart even more.

Charles was so humorous and there was never a dull moment with him. We built a great friendship and fell in love. We became inseparable. His friends would tease him and ask me, what did I do to their friend? He did not want to hang out with the guys like before. One of my co-workers invited us to her party and she kept trying to get us to mingle and dance with other people. Neither of us was interested, she finally gave up trying to convince us, and just walked away shaking her head.

During one of our conversations, I mentioned to him that my mom had an arch at the front gate entrance and the arch was covered with roses. I expressed how much I loved roses. He started buying me roses, picking roses from family and friends yard and eventually planted roses for me.

In 1976 Charles asked me to go on vacation with him to Florida. I teased him about driving the Electra 225. Well, he drove the Electra 225 and we made it safe. We stayed in Panama City Beach, Florida but visited Fort Lauderdale and other parts of the Florida. Our plan was to go to Miami, but we fell in love with Panama City. It was quiet and clean plus the hotel was new. This was just what I needed! When we went back to Texas, I was refreshed and ready to make some major decisions. In that same year, I was still 19 years old. I bought a car and a house as my father-in-law had suggested.

In 1977-He asked me to marry him, once his divorce was final. But we came to an agreement to wait a little longer. Charles played baseball, Shawn and I were at most of the games. She would cheer him on by saying, go my Charles! Go my Charles! Meanwhile, The court date was set to finalize the divorce and visitation with his children was settled.

His ex left the kids outside the courthouse, and he went back in to let the judge know he would take the kids home with him and would not leave them alone in front of the courthouse. He brought them home and came into the house to let me know what happened and to ask me if it was ok for them to stay with us until he or they got in touch with their mom. I said sure and made room for everyone to have a place to sleep. The next morning, his daughters left early. The youngest boy and the oldest stayed for a few days. The younger boy was the last to leave. His mom came with the police one night while Charles was at work to pick him up.

A few days later, prior to Charles's sons leaving, I went to visit Drew's aunt on my way to work. This was a regular stop when I worked since the apartment complex was close to my job. As I was leaving, I saw Charles oldest daughter at the apartment complex with a couple of young people with her and she asked me where was her brothers?

I said they're home and she called me out of my name and said, That's not their home! I said it is for now. I must admit, I clapped back and did the same, I didn't want this to continue so I back out of the parking lot and drove off. A few seconds later I heard something hit my window on the driver's side and I thought it might be kids throwing rocks. I put my car in reverse to see what happened. My cousin-in-law, Kerry, was screaming as my car window on the driver's side shattered into pieces. I saw this frightful look on Kerry's face as she called out my name and asked if I was okay. I said yes and started to tell her that some kids probably threw rocks at my window. She said no it was Charles's daughter. I saw her pull the gun out and point it at your car, once she shot the gun, she and her friends ran. Since they lived in the same apartment complex, Kerry knew who she was. I was shocked that she would go that far. I hated going home to tell Charles what happened. He was hurt and disappointed and didn't want to believe that she did that. I decided to press charges, a date was set, and I went to juvenile court. She was put on probation and had to pay or reimburse me to get a new window installed. A few days later, I was leaving work and my car wouldn't start. I called Charles to come meet me. Someone had put sugar in my gas tank. For several months I didn't know what to expect, it was always some kind of attack whether it was virtual or physical, It was draining.

The following year in December during the Christmas holidays someone rang the doorbell. It was Thomesa at the door with her baby girl. She asked if she could come in and asked me to forgive her. I said she was forgiven and welcomed her into our home again. She came to visit off and on. She allowed us to spend time with the baby until she was toddler age as did Charles younger daughter with her first-born son. We enjoyed the time with the grandkids when they came over. I took them to Church with me when they came on the weekends.

Throughout the years, the visits were regular for a short time and then there was a period when we wouldn't see anyone. When we moved to California, we talked on the phone sometimes. When visited one time we stayed at one of Charles's daughters and broke bread with them. It was a nice visit.

During the late 70's, there were couples that hung out together, Ella & Ed, Chris & John, Wanda & Harold, Charles & I. Once Linda married Robert, they joined us as we celebrated holidays together, we had candlelight dinners at each other's house. We even convinced our husbands to wear tuxedos while we wore evening gowns. I always had this event planning mind wanting to do something elegant and exciting. Chris was all in with me and then we both would convince the others. We didn't go to clubs, we celebrated at home. Our kids played together and knew wherever we were they had to clean up before we left and put away the toys. On most Friday nights there was a party at Ella & Ed's house. There was always music & dancing, the kids joined us when it was time to dance. It was so much fun! The kids and adults still reminisce about it today.

We invited other couples when we went to Sartin's, an all-you-can-eat seafood buffet restaurant. They specialized in barbecue crabs; I only like fish and shrimps, but the shrimps were the last dish they brought. I was so hungry by this time.

In 1978 I found out I was pregnant. I had a miscarriage prior to this pregnancy. Charles and I were excited about the unexpected news. I had the flu when I was four months, after it passed, I started craving a juicy watermelon which was not in season, but Kroger still sold them. At midnight my brother Kenneth took a ride to Kroger to purchase a watermelon.

In July 1978, my eighth month, a drunk driver hit the front end of the car real hard and kept going.

I just sat in the car, scared to move. I was thinking...I've come too far in this pregnancy to lose this baby. A couple of men that saw the accident came to the car to push it out of the middle of the road and into the nearest parking lot. People rushed to the car to see if I was okay. Someone said, oh she's pregnant! Another asked, "Are you okay"? I burst into tears, and said I hope so.

They started to open the car door to help me out. I didn't want to move in fear of seeing blood. One person went inside the restaurant to call the paramedics and I asked them to call Charles. He arrived before I went to the hospital. Everything checked out okay with me and the baby.

On the morning of August 8, 1978, I was preparing Charles lunch for work, I experienced some cramping and mentioned it to Charles. He asked me if I thought it was labor, I told him I wasn't sure so go to work, it would be okay.

Meanwhile, he called his nephew Clint and told him to be on standby.

Clint kept in touch with me and decided it was best to leave by 10:00 am to be on our way to John Sealy in Galveston. That was the fastest ride to Galveston that I had ever experienced. We made it safe; Clint informed the ER staff what was happening.

I had to wait for a bit, but once there was a free bed, they brought me up to labor and delivery. Later that afternoon I convinced Clint to go home, since he called Charles and gave him the updates.

The doctor said it would be a while before delivery since I was dilating slowly even though they induced labor. Charles arrived around 6:00pm. The labor pains had increased by this time. He held my hand and watched the monitor so he could tell when I was in pain. We had an excellent team of doctors and nurses. When it got closer, Sandy was one of the nurses that I connected with because of her compassion. She announced, it's time to take you down to delivery. She teased Charles because he sounded so sure of himself, that the baby was a boy. Our baby girl was born at 7:00pm. Sandy met Charles in the hallway so he could see the baby. She had her eyes closed and he said, open your eyes for your daddy! She opened her eyes and there was loud laughter outside of the delivery room. One of his friends was with him and there were nurses, so he had witnesses.

Charles was so proud and shared the story with family and friends. He came to my room to tell me what happened and handed me a piece of paper with the name he selected for our daughter (Charlette Yvette). I changed the spelling to Charlotte. Shawn, Charles and I talked to the baby while she was in my belly regularly, so she would recognize our voices. When I found out I was pregnant Shawn was 5 years old. I made sure I took her to a lot of my appointments so she could hear the baby heartbeat. I allowed her to feel the kicks and encouraged her to talk to the baby so she/he would know big sister's voice. Holding her baby sister for the first time brought her so much joy! Those special moments and helping mom were all good, until Charlotte turned one. She wasn't having the I'm the big sister talks or big sister giving her orders.

Charlotte was 5 lbs. and ½ ounce. The doctor said her skin was a little yellow and he believed it was jaundice. He decided to keep her for a few days for testing. At first, he suggested that I leave her for a week and come back to pick her up. I said, if she's staying, I am too! This was on a Tuesday; we both were home by the weekend. Everyone was waiting to see our baby girl, so there were visitors most of the weekend. One of my neighbors, Pat was so sweet, she came over with a delicious plate of food, and was so satisfying after eating hospital food.

Charles and I were together six years before we got married. The plan was for a small wedding with 25 guests. I was not sure how that would work since most of his family was in town. I had a large family, but not everyone was in Texas. Charles and I both had a lot of friends.

Our Wedding Day

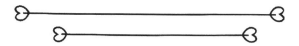

On July 11, 1981, Charles & I were married in our backyard. It rained most of the day and there was some flooding. Our backup plan was a small church, but I really wanted an outside wedding, so I held on to hope. The water settled near the fences of our neighbors on each side. The right side where the chairs went, and the left side where the food tables went were dry.

As I watched the florist's artistic work through my bathroom window, I was amazed at how he blended the pink & lilac with the green background. I chose lilac & pink for my colors even though I would have preferred royal purple and hot pink. My dress was pink, handkerchief style with long lace sleeves.

I couldn't find what I wanted so I bought a long dress that I liked and had it cut and altered. I wore baby breath in my hair instead of a veil. My shoes were pink stilettos. My maid of honor had a lavender and purple handkerchief style dress,

I had four hosts who wore pink, my two daughters who were 3 & 8 wore pink dresses with attached cancan slips and there were bells on each side of the slips. The men & boys wore grey suits and pink shirts. My dad was there, but my oldest brother, Lernest gave me away this time. I wanted Kenneth to sing with his classmate & my friend Wentrice, but he was married, and his wife wasn't too keen on that idea. Wentrice sang **"With You I'm Born Again"** by Billy Preston and Syreeta.

Charles's sisters made dirty rice, potato salad, beans and we purchased the meat and brought it to Charles's cousin who owned a barbecue place, and he barbecued the meat. At one point, the hosts that served the food called me to the side to say they weren't sure if we had enough food. Well, it all worked out, we had more than enough and a lot of leftovers even after people took plates home.

The wedding was so beautiful with over 200 guests. Our theme was **"God Is Love"** The majority of our wedding gifts was money as Charles requested, lol. We didn't need anything for the house. The money was to apply toward our honeymoon. We thought after everyone left, we would enjoy the backyard, play music and dance but there was one guest that would not leave. We threw all kinds of hints; he still didn't get it. Charles finally said man, we're headed to bed since we have an early flight in the morning.

Our honeymoon was in Los Angeles & Diamond Bar California. We also spent a few days in Vegas with my sisters Evelyn & Judy and their husbands who celebrated their anniversaries. We had a blast! We even had a chance to enjoy my brother Nolan in concert.

In the early spring of 1982, several laborers crossed my path, and several witnessed to me about Jesus. I thought I had to clean up my act before coming to Jesus. One day my brother Kenneth drove me to the credit union, my youngest daughter who was almost 4 yrs. old was in the back seat. As we were exiting the freeway, I noticed the car started to speed up, I looked over at Kenneth and I said, press on the brakes!

He said I cannot, the brakes are not working! I told him to blow the horn so that people could know we were coming through. As we were approaching the intersection, the light turned red for us and green for the others. As Kenneth pressed the brakes as hard as he could, we ran through the red light, flashes of my life flowed through my mind as we hit one car and that car hit another, the car spun around, *and we ended up under the freeway after hitting a large post.*

There was broken glass flying inside the car, mostly in the back seat where Charlotte was. Once the car stopped moving, I looked to my left and saw Kenneth was not hurt, I called out to Charlotte (my baby girl), Are you okay? I was so glad to hear that little voice say, mama, I am okay. I was so afraid to get out of the car to check on the people in the other cars that were involved in the accident. I feared the worst. We sat in the car for a few minutes in unbelief of what had just happened and that we were unharmed.

I finally got out of the car to go check on everyone involved. I was so grateful that no one was injured. The cars suffered all the damage. Kenneth decided to find a pay phone to call Charles to let him know what happened while Charlotte and I along with several people in an open field waiting for the police.

While I was waiting, a lady came and stood beside me asking what happened? After I shared, she then said, "Today is the day of your salvation"! She began to share how my life was spared and I needed to accept Jesus as Lord & Savior.

I was finally ready to listen and did not want to run as this powerful witness shared the gospel and prayed for me. When Kenneth returned, I shared with him about the lady who shared the gospel with me. I looked for her but could not find her.

Our lives as we knew it changed drastically in 1982. If you have ever seen the movie called "The Case for Christ". This was very similar to my daily life after I accepted Jesus as Lord and Savior. If you haven't seen the movie yet, please watch it. Charles wasn't an Investigative Journalist or atheist, like Lee Strobel, even though I wondered at times. He was intelligent and had a very sharp intellect. He loved reading, he studied the bible, the history of it and read many commentaries.

He could tell you almost everything he read word for word. Before I came to the Lord, Charles started reading the bible regularly and wanted to share what he read with everyone that visited our home during that time. At one point, I thought he would be saved first. Of course, people shared the gospel with him as people did with me during that time.

In that same year, Texaco Refinery where Charles worked, went on a 7-month strike. While the union negotiated on their behalf, Charles did construction work and whatever work he could find until the strike was over. We were in a financial battle, behind with our bills, with God's provision we were able to keep the lights, water & gas on during the strike because God moved on people's hearts to give.

In 1983- We sold the house I bought, and we decided to buy a house in both of our names. It was a nice size yard where the kids could still have their swing set. The kitchen had just been remodeled with new appliances. We were thankful that we were able to sell the house in one weekend showing. God turned the situation around in our favor when we thought that it might be a foreclosure if the strike continued. Ella & Chris came over to help unpack and decorate. Ella was good at hanging the pictures and Chris was good at hanging the curtains. We stayed up all night. Our husbands hung out together and helped with the handy work and heavy lifting. We always had so much fun together and they both were always ready to help at times like these.

My dad came from Lake Charles to visit more often, Shawn and Charlotte loved their papa. I loved seeing him and Charles together; they both had a great sense of humor and made each other laugh. Watching them laugh together brought joy to me. My dad and I had come a long way from my teenage years when I was bitter toward him after losing my mom and not getting the attention or love I craved from him. I came to a point where I chose to forgive him, and God put a love in my heart for my dad like I never had before. Dad had this bad cough and I noticed there was blood in the bathroom sink sometimes when my dad came to visit. We were told dad started smoking when he was 9 years old while working in the field. He would roll tobacco in the cigarette paper back then. I'm not sure if the uncle that raised him smoked.

In March 1986- One of his friends found him lying on the bathroom floor, called 911 and contacted his sister living next door and three other sisters that were in the same area. My aunt called to let me, and Ella know. We packed and left as soon as we could. We didn't know how long we would be there. The doctor's diagnosis was emphysema, heart attack and possible stroke. When we arrived at the hospital dad had tubes all over, a fan blowing directly on him. He could not speak; his breathing was shallow, and you could hear the wheezing as he struggled to breathe. It made you not want to smoke or stop if you were smoking. It was painful to watch. Ella & I shared the gospel with dad and read the word daily. He still could hear us. I asked him if he wanted to accept Jesus as Lord and he squeezed my hand and blinked his eyes meaning yes. We prayed with him. Tears rolled down his face when I said, I love you daddy! I also said I forgive you dad and I'm sorry for my rebellion and disrespect. I needed his forgiveness as well. He only lived a few days after the heart attack. Ella and I went back home to Beaumont to prepare for family coming in from California. There were a total of 13 people staying at our house. Charles never had a problem in giving our bedroom to family members that came over to visit.

Charles had a friend that had an RV, so he asked him to drive us to Lake Charles for the memorial and funeral services. It was large enough to fit everyone comfortably. The repast was at Aunt

Edith's house (one of my dad's sisters). There was music, singing pictures and a lot of laughter as always when my family came together. It was time to head back to Beaumont, since the Californians would be leaving in a couple of days. It was a wonderful time together even though it was a sad occasion.

Move Preparation

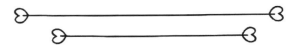

In 1987, Texaco refinery and other oil and gas industries laid off several employees. After much prayer, fasting and seeking the Lord. Charles and had several discussions We decided to sell our home and move to California since there were no openings at refineries nearby. He wanted to move to Salt Lake City, Utah since he lived there when he was younger. I did not want to move there. It was hard to leave my church family in Beaumont. My daughters and I were there for 5 years, we were a tight-knit group. I was involved in children's ministry, prison ministry, greeter, witnessing in our community, Women's prayer group, or whatever area needed to be covered.

My sister & I chaperoned a youth ministry trip etc. My sister and I were part of a small prayer group with women that stood in the gap for their husbands. We prayed on Fridays and alternated homes. There were six of us, 3 were separated, and 3 of us were with our husbands. We became so close, we encouraged one another, we cried together, laughed, went out for lunch, and dinner, and had sleepovers. We rented a van and drove to Houston to John Olsteen church for a marriage seminar. We wanted to learn all we could about praying for our husbands to be saved and for us to be the wives God was calling us to be. We all accepted Jesus before our husbands. Our pastor's wife led an women's bible study on Thursdays.

One Thursday, I had a tooth abscess with a lot of pain and swelling. It was hard to open my mouth without experiencing excruciating pain. After talking to my sister and being encouraged, she said you don't know God might heal you. I said you're right! I'm going believing that He will. As Pastor Marilyn was teaching, I can't remember what the message was about, but it was always good. At one point, it was if I was in the room alone. I saw a bright light that was blinding, I covered my eyes. I could see the light was headed in my direction.

At this time, I felt heat penetrating on the side of my face where it was swollen and in pain from the abscess. God's presence was so strong, I started weeping and couldn't stop. Everyone wanted to know what was going on, I could hear them talking but it was like in the background, far away from me. They explained later that they felt God's presence but not like I described. It was so personal. I went expecting and He met me there.

Pastor Marilyn continued with the bible study until I could share. All I could say was, He touched me! He touched me! I wept almost till the end of the bible study. After bible study, I was able to share that I was in pain because of the tooth abscess, and I came by faith believing that I would be heal.

There were so many times that I experienced God's presence during prayer, worship, service, and bible study. I dreaded when I had to go back to the earthly concerns. Psalm 16:11- You will show me the path of life; In your presence is fullness of joy; at Your right hand are pleasures forevermore.

Before we moved to California, the ladies and other church members gave me a farewell party. They shared memories of me. One memory was about how I would invite everyone to lunch or coffee, but because I changed purses often to match my outfits, everyone learned to ask me if I transferred my wallet & checkbook to the purse or if I would be borrowing money to pay for our meal, lol. Another memory was how sensitive I was in God's presence. I would cry uncontrollably. They joked that Kleenex was not enough and brought me a couple of packs of double rolls of bath tissue. After hearing how many lives were touched because Jesus changed my life.

I cried because I had no idea how my life, my faith & Joy in the Lord affected others. The closing song by the worship team was **"Friends are Friends Forever" by Michael W. Smith.**

The plan was for my daughters and me to join Charles in California once our house was sold. We moved with my sister & her husband for a couple of months. We spent most of our time with our church family. God tore down walls in my life during these five years, but there was more to go. I experienced the power of God's love through this body of believers.

Charles went ahead of us to look for work. He applied at a couple of refineries. No doors were opening in his line of work, he became discouraged. He started noticing that there were few places hiring men over 40 years old in the positions that he desired. He was a provider, so he continued searching until he found something, even though It was not the salary he hoped for.

While preparing to move to California and seeking God for direction, I heard Him say, stay home and study my word. He confirmed it with **Jeremiah 31:5-**And I will give you shepherds after my own heart, who will lead you with knowledge and understanding.

Once my daughters and I arrived in California in May 1987-Charles had made special plans for me and him to get away for a couple of days. It had been two months since we seen each other. He booked us a room at a hotel in Palos Verdes, California (one of the wealthiest areas in California) It was breathtaking, to say the least.

We ate well and rode around viewing the beautiful sigh ts. Charles was like a kid when he wanted to surprise me, it was hard for him to keep it to himself. Once we got back to my sister's house. We spent time with our children and family.

I made up my mind since I was back in California, I would take advantage and enroll in a community college or technical school to further my education so that I could get a good-paying job. My brother-in-law brought a flyer home one day and I decided to check it out. It was a technical school in Los Angeles. I enrolled in a Computer Administration Course which included Accounting 1 & 2, Computer 1 & 2 (learning how to operate & utilize a computer in a corporate office setting), Typing 1 & 2, and Office Procedures (English, grammar) I went to school from 8:00 am to 3:00 pm daily.

My typing Instructor put me in charge of the school newsletter, he also allowed me to post a prayer in the weekly newsletter. It was more difficult than I thought it would be going to school, studying and having homework every night and caring for two daughters and my husband. Trying to make sure that I spent time with each of them.

We found an apartment close to Charles's job. We only had one car at the time, so Charles rode the bus to work, and I used the car for school. I led two of my classmates to the Lord. These ladies came up to me wanting to know how they can be saved. My computer instructor didn't care for me & my beliefs. He saw one of my friends crying when I was praying with her and he said, what kind of God makes a person cry? I tried to explain that when you're in the presence of the Lord, you will cry. I'm not sure what his religion was, but he said we never speak his name, we just point upwards to the sky. He watched me daily and when he asked questions, God gave me the answers, but he was not satisfied. My friend Susanne tried to defend me. There were attacks against my faith, but the greatest thing was that God gave me favor in that season.

    I graduated from NTS in 1988, My husband and daughters were at my graduation ceremony. I was so excited, it was a tough year, but God bought me through! I started working at the school as an Administrative Assistant to the **Director of**

Education. I was offered the position before I graduated. The job was challenging, but I loved working for Jerome. He challenged me, he was a perfectionist and loved making corrections with his favorite red pen. Sometimes, I just wanted to throw all the red pens away, lol. No matter how many times I thought to myself, he will not find any mistakes this time! He always found a mistake and he would circle it with his red pen. Overall, he meant well, he challenged my capabilities, and it brought out my talents.

He trusted me and left me alone in the office to manage the instructors that he was over. I never liked being the only woman working around a lot of men, it made me feel uncomfortable. This position required that I do. All the men were very respectful, so it turned out well. Jerome even allowed me to hire a friend that graduated with me as my assistant. She was going through a tough time, her husband was filing for a divorce, and she didn't have a job.

Jerome would go on these long lunch breaks and would come back drunk. I was so concern about him getting in trouble with his boss the president of the school.

After several occasions, Jay the president of the school came by the office to see Jerome. He avoided Jay as much as he could until the day came when Jay fired him. I wondered if I would be fired shortly after. Jay's executive assistant, Iliana, didn't think I had enough experience to be the Director of Education's assistant. God gave me favor with Jay, Jerome, and the Instructors. I worked alone and supervised the instructors. I wasn't going to quit; I was still getting a paycheck. Once day Judy who was the administrative assistant to Jerome's wife in the home school department came by and noticed that I was still working. She said, Deborah you're still here? I said yes, nobody fired me or told me I had to leave. She said, you shouldn't be here by yourself. I was perfectly fine, by myself. She said,

"I will talk to Marilyn and see if you can come work with us on the home school side." Well within a few days, I was working for Marilyn in accounts payable and receivable. Once she left for a business trip, the Director of Sales thought it would be okay for me to work for him since his assistant was out indefinitely. I enjoyed working for him, he was a mild-mannered man.

When he left for a business trip, I was moved to home school admissions department where I shared a cubicle with a buddhist. It was all smiles until she realized I wouldn't be converted to her beliefs. She named movie stars who believed in buddha thinking that would impress me. When she shared her beliefs, I felt like the door was open for me to share my beliefs about Jesus dying on the cross for our sins. We were back-to-back in the cubicle. Some days were like Elijah battling Baal (1 Kings17:1-19:21). Some of my candidates would speed peak of God's goodness and then I started to share my story how God saved me and how He's working in my life. It could get loud as we praised God. Meanwhile, Lavelle was trying to convince candidates that buddha was the way. She also got loud sometimes, there were quite a few times that she stomped out headed to the restroom chanting. My co-workers would tease me and say, Deborah what did you do to Lavelle? I was glad when my assignment ended in that department.

I was moved to the switchboard next and filled in for the cashier when she was off until Lee the President of the Home School division sent his executive assistant to let me know that he was impressed with my skills and that he received good reports about me. He wanted me to know that he was aware of my graduation and degree. He wanted me to work in a position that was suited for me. Eventually, I had a choice, and I went back to Marilyn in the accounting department since I did take Accounting 1 & 2. It was a stressful department. When the bills was past due in the accounts I managed, the company called to speak to me and wanted to know when to expect payments. They didn't care to hear the president hasn't approved or signed the check. I was the one that the clients took it out on, It was so stressful. The company never seemed to pay their bills on time. After a while, I saw that accounting was not for me because I couldn't deal with being stressed over my bills and the company bills too. After that experience, I never wanted to work in accounting again.

1989-I filled out an application at USC and was offered a position in Admissions. I decided to accept to get my foot in the door. My friend in HR told me it was temporary until other positions open with my supervisor was a bitter middle-aged woman, who was verbally & emotionally abusive to her employees. Most of them were under psychiatric care. When I heard some of their stories, I couldn't believe it.

It was like we were in elementary school and had to raise our hands to go to the restroom. I remember going to the restroom one day and one of the ladies said, you must ask Estelle before stepping away from your desks. I said I'll just get in trouble because I'm not sitting here waiting until she returns. She didn't say much to me, she just observed me as I observed her.

I heard her telling one of the Hispanic ladies that she's needs to go back to Mexico, and she continued to tear into her. The young lady held her head down, before I knew it, I was defending her and letting Estelle know how offensive & painful her words were. She got terribly upset with me and told me to mind my own business. I let her know that it was unacceptable and that I would not put up with her talking to me in that same manner. No one spoke up to her. After that incident she respected me.

I reported the incident to Human Resources and was told that there were several complaints over the years but those over her never did anything about it. There were no consequences for her actions. Thank God I only worked in admissions for only a short while until the position in financial aid became available.

God kept me and gave me favor in many areas, but it was no way of getting around the battles but through prayer. I woke early for my prayer time before work and prayed with the girls before they went to school. This was a must! A door opened in financial aid and my HR contact asked me if I was interested in a Data Entry position. Within a couple of days, I was working in Financial Aid and in training. I was excited for a new opportunity.

Disobedience and Church Drama

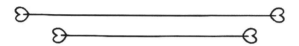

I didn't wait on God to lead me to the right church. I visited several churches thinking God would let me know which one was the right one. One church I went to just to be in church, the greeters were distant and unfriendly, totally different than what I was used to in Texas. I chalked it up to how different people were in California, not friendly as southerners. It got to a point at this church, where I was not allowed to praise God freely. If I would put one foot outside my row because I needed space to lift my hands without hitting the person next to me, an usher would be there motioning me to put my feet in row. Within a couple of months, I started to feel like I was bound in chains. I had to go somewhere I could freely praise God. I saw one of my classmates that I led to the Lord, and she began to share about the church she was going to. She shared with excitement the freedom in the atmosphere during worship and praise. I wanted to experience God's presence as I had before during worship and praise service before moving to California.

I decided to visit the church, it was different as night and day from the previous church. The service was on Saturday evening instead of Sunday. I was just excited to Praise God freely again. I served in children's church, mostly in the nursery working with the babies, I joined the older adult prayer group who specifically prayed for the pastoral staff and their family. Once I met Ursula who became a friend, and we are still friends today. We started spending a lot of time together and our two younger daughters would spend time together sometimes. Sharing & talking to her became a safe place for me once I felt like I could trust her. She lived 5-10 minutes away from my place. If Ursula or I missed church on the same day, we were questioned why? Where were you? Shawn was in the youth group and most of the children been there from the beginning. She felt left out like she didn't fit in. I tried to give the kids the benefit of the doubt, and she was misreading the situation. As time went on, I saw so many things out of order because of the leadership. Older adult prayer meetings were once a week.

I overheard a conversation at one of the meetings that some of the ladies were having. It was about how the church had been fasting and praying for another pastor's fall because the pastor at this church and the other pastor had some disagreements years ago. I said, what? They said oh you didn't know. I said no I wouldn't come into agreement with that kind of prayer knowingly! The Lord was slowly uncovering things. Once I knew, I couldn't stay in the prayer group. The Lord let me know I would be held accountable since I knew. I eventually left that church as God begin to expose more secrets.

Wolves In Sheep's Clothing

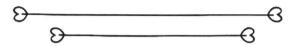

Matthew 7:15 (NLT)- Beware of false prophets who come disguised as harmless sheep but are really vicious wolves.

While working at USC, I prayed in the chapel on the campus a couple of days a week. The warfare was real. One day I met this couple in the chapel along with some ladies praying. They started asking me questions. They asked if I wanted to join them in prayer, I did hesitantly. I didn't see them for a while then one day I went to the chapel and there they were. I prayed with them on that day, but I had to get back to work since

I was on my lunch break. One of the ladies ran after to me to let me know about the days they had bible study. Going to church, bible study, and prayer meetings was a way of escape from my home life at the time. My defense was up with this group, I had just left a church who was fasting and praying for another pastor's fall. I always loved fasting and praying because I had seen God move mightily when I did. That is when I was around my foundational church group in Texas. The churches my daughters and I visited a couple of months after we moved into our own place were so Hollywood-like. It appeared as if the leaders were auditioning for a part in a movie. Oh, how I missed southern hospitality!

This couple that I prayed with in the chapel was from Texas. At one of the meetings, I met two ladies who I connected with. They both worked on USC campus also. I went out to lunch with them at times. I asked them if they knew of a Christian person that did income taxes. One of the ladies told me that the guy we prayed with in chapel did her taxes. She encouraged me to give it a try. I was hesitant because I didn't want him to think if he did my taxes that I would become a member of their church group. Just before the deadline to file taxes, I contacted him and scheduled a meeting. My walls were up, just in case they tried to pressure me about becoming a member of their church group.

He and his wife could feel my walls of defense because I had a tone in my voice when I answered their questions. After he did my taxes, she asked me to join her in the living room. She asked if I had anything against her, I told her I have not had good experience with church folks in California. She said she understood since she was not from California. After this, I didn't see them for at least a couple of months. I decided to attend one of their bible studies at the home of one of their members. The message was powerful and seemed to line up with scriptures, but I didn't go every week.

The heat of the fiery trial I was facing at home became so overwhelming I just wanted to scream, and I did when I took long rides by myself. I felt there was no safe place to share what I was going through until I met my friend Ursula. Sharing with my sisters was not the solution, too many emotions and not enough wisdom. I needed an objective view. As Charles battled with his issues, not being the main provider, having a hard time accepting the woman that he married the year before had changed after she accepted Jesus as her Lord and Savior. We both were dealing with how we were unequally yoked, growing apart in our marriage and our family life. These trials caused him to turn to alcohol more and it caused me to bend my knees and pray more. I started to dread the weekends because I knew it was going to end in an argument.

I started going to the bible studies regularly in need of fellowship and the word. It was called "Ministry of Reconciliation" It started out good, so eventually I invited family and friends to bible studies. I didn't want to commit to join yet. Later when I became a member, we would hit the streets of Los Angeles to witness and share the gospel. We organized a mission and food pantry. Everyone donated food and clothing for the poor and homeless. One of the members allowed us to use her garage since it was in a central location. I oversaw inventory and replenishing by requesting donations from members as needed. We went out witnessing every weekend and invited the homeless to come back with us to eat and freely shop if they needed food or clothing. I was so excited to see people coming to the Lord. Most of the women that were married, their husbands were not saved. Some were separated or divorced. Most of us were having marriage and family issues.

  The leaders remind me of Job's three friends who spent 7 days with him to comfort him after they heard of his suffering. After the seven days, they were hurling accusations and condemning him. When you first came to them, they appeared to be so kind and compassionate about everyone's situation, which made you feel like you could trust them with your vulnerability. It was all good for a short season, then they would start to say these things are happening to you because you have sin in your life and you're evil. When they finished tearing you down, you felt defeated and hopeless. Just when you thought after you repented, you're on the right track again. You were ripped to shreds with verbal abuse and accusations again.

I threatened to leave Charles many times throughout the years. When we lived in Texas, I would go stay a few days with my aunt in Lake Charles, Louisiana. He would call every day asking when I was coming home. I was gone for 2 weeks at a time. I left for three months in California before the big move. He pleaded with me to come back home. After that Charles came to the bible studies a couple of times and even went up for prayer to be saved one of those times. For a short time, we prayed together, had discussions about the bible without any debating.

I really hoped that this was the end of dreadful drunken weekends with arguments and accusations. After trying for a couple of more years, I finally realized it would not end well if I stayed any longer. I told him months before that if left again this time I wouldn't come back. I tried to focus on scriptures, 1 Corinthians 7:14- For the unbelieving husband is sanctified by the husband; else were your children unclean; but now they are holy, but if the unbeliever leaves let him do so. 1 Corinthians 7:16 (NIV)- How do you know, wife, whether you will save your husband? Or, how do you know, husband, whether you will save your wife?

My (youngest daughter) Charlotte & I left while he was at work one night. My oldest daughter had already moved out by this time. Just like Charles wondered where the woman was, he fell in love with, I wondered the same thing. Where was this man that I loved because of his big heart, that cherished me and would do anything to keep our family together. We were separated for ten years; within that time, I filed for a divorce. I went through depression during, and I started seeing a Christian therapist who was such a blessing to me. I looked forward to my weekly visits. It was like I was going to visit a friend. Sandy helped me through some rough times.

Charlotte and I were in this ministry of reconciliation group. It seemed normal and fun in the beginning or for the first 2-3 years. We moved around a bit but always stayed with a member of the group until I started helping the leaders take care of foster kids that they brought into their home. At one point, there was a ten-month-old baby, I helped care for her and another baby for a while until she went back to her biological mom. Then later 2 other toddlers came, a brother & a sister. We were not on good terms at this time, but they knew how I felt about the foster children. They made a special trip to bring the kids where I was living as they requested my help to work alongside with them take care of these abused kids. When I heard the kids' story, it was hard to say no. Most of the kids had been sexual abused or the mother was on drugs when she carried them. My daughter stayed with my sister for a while. To think at one time a couple of us mothers gave our permission for the leader to discipline our children. We were deceived in thinking they really cared about our children. The thing about my relationship with these people was that I didn't always follow their commands or orders, and this irritated them. They put me out a lot. While living with any of the members, they would go back and report my activity within their house to the leaders. One thing I despised was, when they called, they would put you on the speaker so they both would talk to you at once. Most of the time, it was about something they heard about you. I was never one to hide my feelings or emotions when I didn't like something or disagreed.

Being in their house was the worst. Whatever you thought you knew was all incorrect according to them. Things like washing dishes, cleaning, cooking, running bath water, putting the shower curtain in or out etc. were all wrong. No matter how hard you tried to do right, it was wrong! Somedays, I would shut down and couldn't go to take care of the kids. They had to get my sister or someone else. They were so hard on the foster kids especially with the verbal abuse. They were verbally, emotionally, and spiritually abusive to everyone that was there. There was no sexual abuse that we know of. Once the husband-and-wife cult leaders encouraged the women to leave their husbands even if they weren't verbal or physically abusive (which was not a fact in some cases) then the ladies were accused of wanting her husband. Everything we shared about your past, or what you were going through was used against you as a weapon. Like a narcissistic relationship. They spoke curses over people's lives regularly. Charlotte left California when she was 18 years old and moved to Texas to be with her sister and her dad. I was still there for 5 more years, but living with outside roommates that were not members of the cult. The cult members invited me to walk with them on a 6-to-10-mile walks occasionally, until I ended that. I begin to enjoy my freedom on the outside so much, going and coming as I pleased without accusations and ungodly counsel.

Later they started a home health agency and contacted me to ask if I wanted to work for them. At the time, I loved being free and on my own. I bought me a computer and a cellphone. My credit was excellent, so I was approved for all major credit cards. I was working a regular 8:00-5:00 job, and I had my own cleaning business. Life was good. At one time, I was a Certified Nurse's Assistant, so they knew I had the experience. One of the members was a nurse. I also loved caring for the elderly as I did with the foster kids, and they knew this too. I told them I liked what I was doing, and I was making good money. The male leader pressed and told me how I would be helping these people. I finally said I'll get back to you. I didn't but they called me back. I finally said yes. I told myself I was living on the outside and I still had freedom. I decided to focus on the patients as I did with the foster kids.

I had a chance to travel with one of the patients (a doctor and his wife). We went to Palm Springs a couple of times, also to San Diego for 4 days for a family wedding. For some reason, the couple was comfortable with my driving and the doctor's wife was sharp on directions otherwise we would be lost. They always paid for my own private suite and meals. The best part of it was after the trip, I could go to a place called home that was not connected to the cult. My roommate Luiz at the time was a kind compassionate woman who was hardly home. Not like the first roommate who was from Iran and had some serious mental issues. Every patient had a different need, some cases were harder than others, but it all balanced out and was a blessing overall. This one patient would call my name most of the night. I look forward as she did to going for a walk on the beach.

I remember asking God one day, Lord have I learned all that I was supposed to learn in this situation? I believe you have a purpose and a plan in everything you allow to come into my life. I knew one thing; I didn't want to be bitter in my heart toward these cult leaders. I knew God would have the final say in the long run and he would judge.

The Cult's Deceptive Plan
(some quotes taken from psychology today magazine)

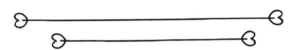

A cult is a group or movement held together by a shared commitment to a charismatic leader or ideology. It has a belief system that has the answers to all of life's questions and offers a special solution to be gained only by following the leader's rules.

Cults often take advantage of vulnerable people in search of comfort and identity; they disable critical thinking processes, freeze emotional processing to both gain, and maintain control over their members.

Who is susceptible to brainwashing?

Someone who is emotionally vulnerable, who suffered abuse or neglect as a child or whose relationship with their family is strained.

The three phases of brainwashing

1) Dependency-The state of relying on or being controlled by someone.
2) Dissonance- Inconsistency between the beliefs one holds or between one's actions and one's beliefs.

Attitude Change-Attitude change is achieved when individuals experience feelings of uneasiness or guilt due to cognitive dissonance, and actively reduce the dissonance through changing their attitude, beliefs, or behavior relating in order to achieve consistency with the inconsistent cognition.

Spiritual Captivity

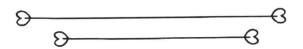

Captive one taken in war. Captives were often treated with great cruelty and indignity (1 Kings 20:32; Joshua 10:24; Judges 1:7; 2 Sam. 4:12; Judges 8:7; 2 Sam 12:31; 1 Chronicles 20:3).

What are the signs of captivity?

Captivity undermines your confidence. You feel as if you can't finish anything. You become apologetic and unsure of yourself. Even when you venture into something new, you have no fruit to show for it.

Jeremiah 29:14

And I will be found of you, saith the LORD: and I

will turn away your captivity, and I will gather you from all the nations, and from all the places whither I have driven you, saith the LORD; and I will bring you again into the place whence I caused you to be carried away captive.

Breaking The Chains Of Spiritual Captivity

Melvin Maughmer Jr.

UNDERSTAND: - Captivity is defined as the state of being captured, imprisoned, detained or held against one's will. It is a state of being demobilized as a result of the forces of darkness. The inability to fulfill one's destiny, the state of operating below the capacity ordained by God, the absence of substantive or identifiable progress in the lives of man, the state of being grind to a halt, lack of capacity to excel in well-being, lack of progress in all ramifications, inability to enjoy good health, or a good marriage. In very case the one that is being held captive is being held or detain by some physical means such as: a prison cell, hand cuffs, shackles, chains, fetters or even by another person.

Spiritual captivity is the state of being captured without any tangible, physical or material evidence of that captivity. However, your life displays all and more of the signs and evidence of one that has been detained or imprisoned due to the inability to succeed or make progress.

To be imprisoned, detained, or captured, firstly, restricts or limits one of their freedoms. Better yet, they can see success, freedom, joy, peace and all things good they desire but do not possess the ability to possess or achieve it because of the obvious; they are being restrained or held against their will.

Even though the definition of captivity is defined as the state of being captured, there exists two types of captivity and they are the **physical captivity** that we see where people are in fetters, chains, handcuffs and then the one that we do not see which is **Spiritual captivity** where people are bound in the confines of the minds. It is this one that we do not see that can be the most challenging and frustrating. Challenging and frustrating because we cannot see what is keeping us from progressing and succeeding. There is nothing visible or has been presented as evidence of this imprisonment or detention, but we know we are bound because of our lack of progress.

Purpose & Identity

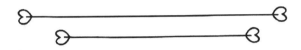

When we experience a major trauma or disappointment or live under a particular negative circumstance for a long time, we tend to become hindered in some area of our lives. We find ourselves changing the truth of the Bible, God's Word, and His ways to match up with our personal experiences. We come under a spirit of captivity because our culture or experience has taught us something that is completely different from the ways of the Spirit of God.

Once a spirit of captivity has taken root in your life, you will start to lose your sense of purpose—perhaps not your entire life's purpose, but some aspect of it. You may be bound by a fear of flying, for example, or by a pattern of persistent anger and abuse.

Though you love God with all your heart, your past may have been so dysfunctional and full of hurt that now you cannot seem to break out of horrible habits developed long ago. Even after evil spirits are cast out of you, your mind must be renewed. In other words, you have to learn a new way of living that is according to God's ways.

For example, if your pattern growing up was that your father could never seem to keep a good job or provide a stable income, then without your realizing it, those years in "Babylon" can lead to similar inconsistency in you. You find yourself going through the years not being able to get ahead in life and thus feeling like a failure without any solid goals.

This is how a spirit of captivity tries to destroy your purpose. You have learned something that is not in line with godliness. The demons may have come and gone, but they have left a permanent imprint on you.

Romans 12:1-2 gives us insight into this revelation and provides some hands-on ways we can change wrong mindsets: "I beseech you therefore, brethren, by the mercies of God, that you present your bodies a living sacrifice, holy, acceptable to God, which is your reasonable service. And do not be conformed to this world, but be transformed by the renewing of your mind, that you may prove what is that good and acceptable and perfect will of God" (NKJV).

False Teachers/False Prophets

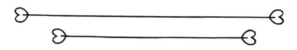

Jeremiah 23:1-4, 21-25 (God led me to Jeremiah 23 after I came out)

"Woe to the shepherds who destroy and scatter the sheep of My pasture!" says the LORD. ² Therefore thus says the LORD God of Israel against the shepherds who feed My people: "You have scattered My flock, driven them away, and not attended to them. Behold, I will attend to you for the evil of your doings," says the LORD. ³ "But I will gather the remnant of My flock out of all countries where I have driven them and bring them back to their folds; and they shall be fruitful and increase. ⁴ I will set up shepherds over them who will feed them; and they shall fear no more, nor be dismayed, nor shall they be lacking," says the LORD.

²¹ "I have not sent these prophets, yet they ran.
I have not spoken to them, yet they prophesied.
²² But if they had stood in My counsel,
And had caused My people to hear My words,
Then they would have turned them from their evil way
And from the evil of their doings.

²³ "*Am* I a God near at hand," says the LORD,
"And not a God afar off?
²⁴ Can anyone hide himself in secret places,
So I shall not see him?" says the LORD;
"Do I not fill heaven and earth?" says the LORD.

God Restored Our Marriage & Our Family

Joel 2:25-And I will restore to you the years that the locust hath eaten, the cankerworm, and the caterpillar, and the palmerworm, my great army which I sent among you.

Meanwhile in 2002 my daughter Charlotte was on a new job back in Houston and her manager told them to play around on the computer to get used to the system. She felt led to type in my name and all my information came up. Thank God for my new gateway computer that I had just purchased, my phone number was listed at the time. Every time I went home, I was on the computer. I didn't go home but once or twice a month since we went from one assignment to another. When I got home there was a message on my phone from my daughters. I called the number that was left on the voicemail. It was Shawn's number (my oldest daughter). I didn't recognize her voice; she had a Texas twang. I left a message and waited to hear back; I was so excited. You are told in the cult once you're separated from your family, that they don't want anything to do with you anymore. If you did talk to anyone in your family, they were there to shadow or coach you. I really thought since it had been almost 6 years since I saw my youngest and at least 10 years since I saw my oldest that they felt abandoned by me and didn't want me in their lives.

I made up my mind after my daughters called me back, that I was going to Houston to reconnect with them and my oldest granddaughter. This was my desire that the enemy tried to bury, but God opened the door. One of the most liberating moments was when I called and left a message on the "cult leaders" voicemail letting them know that

I was not returning to work for them. Later that day I received a voicemail saying how evil I was and how I had this planned all along. My mind was set, let them think whatever they will. I started preparing for my trip, purchasing my ticket since I decided to take Amtrak train there. I thought it would be a nice ride and sometime to pray and think.

    It took 2 days and 3 hours to get there. I met nice people on the train, we had our meals together and our rooms were nearby. I wanted to be there in August since both of my daughters' birthdays were in August. We talked almost every day until I left, I also talked to Davian on the phone, she talked in her baby language. While I was on the train I stayed in contact with my girls. I asked my daughters not to tell their dad I was coming to visit. They assured me if he knew I was coming into town that they would not be able to keep him away.

In August 2002, I made it to Houston Texas. Shawn and her husband at that time, picked me up from the train station. There were smiles and hugs. Shawn was holding Davian, I looked at her and said hi, I'm your grandma. She reached out to me holding her arms up for me to hold her. I knew I could not be a long-distance grandmother and I wouldn't be able to go back to California. Davian's dad used his employee discount at the hotel I was staying at for a couple of days. I wanted to spend alone time with Davian. She was so cuddly and didn't cry at all. Charlotte and Shawn came the next day so we could spend time together.

Charles called them while they were at the hotel, neither of them wanted to answer the phone, they didn't know what to say since it was supposed to be a secret that I was there. He had been looking for them, he had gone to their place, and they weren't there. He wanted to know when they would be home. It was his weekend to spend time with them. I told Charlotte to answer the phone, she said are you sure? He was giving her a hard time about not being home, I said give me the phone. She put her hand over the phone and asked if I was sure, she said moma don't let him pressure you. Once you talk to him, he won't stay away.

I said hello! When he heard my voice on the phone, he was in disbelief. He said, who is this? I said this is Deborah, Shawn & Charlotte's mother. There was silence on the phone. I said, do I need to call 911? He said, you might, lol. He immediately said baby I love you! I said I'm not trying to hear that right now. He changed the subject, so what do you think about our granddaughter? I said, "She's adorable", I'm in love. He said, when can I see you? I said, I don't know yet. Labor Day was coming up on September 2, 2002. Shawn said we could do something for Labor Day at their house. It was the following week, he called to say he was on his way. Shawn heard his truck and shouted, daddy's here!

When he walked through the door, he said, "where's your momma?" I was upstairs doing my hair. He was anxiously waiting when I walked down the stairs. He grabbed me and hugged me so tightly. Again, he said, I love you baby! Wherever I went, there he was. We talked and laughed, and it was a good day. We went to the bowling alley as a group one night and that was fun.

I told Charles I wasn't ready to jump back into anything as of yet. We talked every day after. He shared with me how he was hurt when he came home from work to find that we had left and only his recliner, tv and bedroom set were left in the apartment. I reminded him how I kept asking him to change, but he wouldn't. He said when he finally realized that I was not coming back home this time, he moved back to Beaumont, Texas. He said he cried a lot on the drive back to Beaumont. He listened to Boys to Men song "At the End of the Road" and Toni Braxton song "Unbreak My Heart" and he broke down crying. He said he stopped drinking and smoking without any problem. I remember he didn't want to sign the divorce papers. I contacted his sister and asked her to tell him to please sign so I could get on with my life. He did date someone for a while, but it didn't last. I wasn't interested in dating, plus being in the cult for part of the time, dating wasn't allowed. This was my second marriage and his second, even though mine ended because of death and his ended because of divorce. I had no desire to get married again.

I had invested over 17 years of my life at this time in our relationship and didn't want to start over. We were together 6 years prior to our wedding in 1982 and married 11 years when we separated. We talked openly about our lives and what he and I were going through individually and as a married couple. We hadn't talked about like that since we first met. He kept saying things would be different this time.

I laid down a lot of rules and things that must happen before I can commit again. Counseling was one of the things he had to agree to. We found a Christian counselor that really help us to break the ice and admit to our part in the marriage troubles. We had some good sessions and a lot of laughter because of our sense of humor in sharing some of our issues. The therapist said, "I'm not worried about you two." Because of my trust issues, I tested Charles a lot and to my surprise, he passed all the tests. He was so attentive and sensitive to my emotional needs. When we first got back together, he wasn't sure if I would leave him again and I wasn't sure if he would push me to that point where I wanted to leave again. I had to go back to California to finalize some things and get my computer and furniture. He rented a truck and drove me to California to get my things. He said if God gave him a chance to have me back in his life, he wasn't losing me again. When I tell you God restored my marriage and relationships, He did it completely and it was like no time has been lost.

My daughters and I had some heart-to-heart talks. I listened to them as they shared what they went through when I was absent from their lives. I went to a couple of therapy sessions with Shawn. I asked for their forgiveness, and the hardest part was to forgive myself for not being there for them when they needed me the most. I'm so thankful that Charles was there for Charlotte when she lost her first-born son. This was definitely out of character for me. I tried to be as open as I could with them. It's not always easy to admit when you're wrong.

On July 11, 2003, Charles & I remarried and renewed our vows at the Waterwall in Houston, Texas in the Galleria area. This was the same date we were married in 1981. Only a small group of family & friends were invited. My younger brother and a high school friend sang our original theme song from our 1981 wedding. "With You, I'm Born

Again" by Billy Preston and Syreeta Wright. We also had live music played by young people who were friends of Charlotte. We went out to eat Mexican food with our guests afterwards. On Saturday, July 12, 2003, we had a small reception at Shawn's place.

In 2004 Charles was working as a truck driver, he was delivering a product to a company in Conneaut Ohio, and his back went out while he was lifting a load. He was experiencing debilitating pain when he called me to let me know he was on his way to the hospital. They did CT-Scans & X-rays, gave him something for pain, and Schneider, the trucking company flew him back to Houston.

I set an appointment with one of Memorial Hermann's top back surgeons within a week or so. He was told he needed surgery as soon as possible. Charles continued taking walks around the complex where we lived at the time. One day the muscles in his legs started to tighten up and he could not move.

He was taking too long to come back home, so I went to check where he usually would take his walk. I found him in a lot of pain, and he couldn't walk. Once he rested for 10 mins, he was able to move slowly. We both realized something had to be done. He didn't want to rush into anything, so we got a second opinion. Once it was confirmed by a second surgeon. He consulted with the first surgeon and set the date for his surgery.

Meanwhile, our youngest daughter was pregnant with her second daughter. I was planning her baby shower and helping Charles prepare for surgery. It all worked out while he was home recuperating, our granddaughter was born on April 1, 2004.

I wasn't sure how Charles was going to deal with not being able to go back to work for a while. Our youngest daughter was going to college at night and working in the daytime during her pregnancy. Charles & I helped with our two granddaughters, taking care of the baby, and making sure the 3-year get to and from daycare. Being responsible for the baby gave Charles motivation to recover quicker. We took turns sneaking into the bedroom while she was napping to kiss her. Sometimes I would wake her up just to hold her, lol. She would look at us with the cutest smile that would melt our hearts.

Friday nights were usually our date nights. We kept the kids until Charlotte got home from school. We would listen to smooth jazz music because it was relaxing. Our 3-year-old granddaughter Davian would put on her tutu and ballet shoes and dance for us. Once she was done, she would bow and say, thank you, ladies & gentlemen, thank you very much! We traveled by car with a six-month-old baby and a 3-year toddler to visit our daughter and her husband in San Diego, CA. This was our first road trip with these two granddaughters.

In 2005, Charles had a major heart attack. I was on my way home from the grocery store, and I received a call from him. He said, baby when are you coming home? I told him I was headed home from the Walmart in the neighborhood. He said I'm not feeling good, my chest feels heavy. I immediately thought of my experience with my first husband. I told him it sounded like he was having a heart attack and told him to sit still while I called 911. The paramedics and I arrived at the same time. Charles was very alert, they started examining him and gave him nitroglycerin. They moved quickly to get him down the stairs from the third floor of the apartment complex where we lived at the time. I told Charles I would meet him at the hospital.

When I arrived at the hospital, they did not take me back right away. It seemed like it took forever before a nurse came to take me to the waiting room near the examining room. It was hours before I received an update on his condition. I felt an urgency to pray and again my mind traveled to the night that Drew died. The hospital Chaplin came to the waiting room and asked if he could pray with me. I thanked him and said, please do not take offense sir, but I need to talk to God alone right now. He said, no offense taken, I'm around if you need me. I needed to petition the Lord and cry out to Him. I walked back and forth in that small waiting room asking God to spare Charles's life, saying God I know you have an appointed time for us to be born and a time for us to die, but O' Lord please do not take Charles now. Please give us more time together, Lord I am not ready, Lord, I'm not prepared for this. O' Lord, my God! I am not trying to be disrespectful, but I am pleading and asking for your mercy upon Charles and upon me. I prayed until I felt relief.

After I finished praying, a man from housekeeping came by the waiting room and asked if I was okay. I explained that I had been there for hours, and no one had come to give me an update on my husband's condition. He went to the desk nearby and asked for my husband's name. Once he typed it in, he immediately saw where they had Charles. He said ma'am I found his room; I will take you there.

Right around that time, Dr. Mohammed, an on-call cardiologist that was working on Charles came out of the elevator and walked up to me and introduced himself. He stated that he and another cardiologist could not find the artery that was clogged and stopping his heart. He went on to say, we lost him twice and had to resuscitate him. We finally found the artery that was blocked, it was behind his heart.

He said come quickly, he is in the elevator, and we are taking him to surgery to place a stent in that area. Charles was sitting in a wheelchair in the elevator, he looked up at me and said, hey baby! I was so grateful to see my husband alive. Dr.

Mohammed said, kiss your husband, and I did gladly. Charles did not have a clue about what happened.

The cardiologist was filling in at this hospital for a friend, he had never worked at Memorial Hermann before. He was in a network of cardiologists that was called Alief & West Houston Cardiology which had a hospital attached to the medical offices where he practiced. His shift had just ended at Memorial Hermann, and he was headed out the door when he received an emergency code to return to the hospital S.T.A.T. I saw God's hand in everything when the story came together. The nurse brought me the paperwork to sign and told me she would let me know when the surgery was over and when he was in recovery. The doctors didn't want to put him asleep for the surgery because they didn't want to chance losing him.

The nurse reported that Charles was wide awake through the surgery (angioplasty with stent placement) and he talked the entire time. Lol, that was a good sign, he loved to talk. One of the things we had in common. Once he was discharged from the hospital, we changed some things in our diets. At the time we were living in a senior community that had a fitness center, so he was able to exercise regularly. I went back to work once he was settled at home. Many nights, I went to sleep with my head on his chest near his heart to hear the beautiful sound of his heartbeat. It was music to my ears. I cried and was so grateful to God for giving us more time.

A year later, His cardiologist found blockages in both legs. He suggested bypass surgery immediately. Charles was admitted into the hospital again. The surgery went well, and as a precaution he stayed in the hospital for a week. He stayed in ICU most of his time there so they could keep a close eye on his blood pressure which fluctuated. I stayed in the waiting room while he was there. I only went home to take a shower & eat after visiting him every morning. I wore warm clothes, had a pillow, a blanket, and my laptop & phone. Since visiting hours were only twice a day in ICU, I ranged the buzzer to check on my husband periodically. The cardiologist who assisted the main cardiologist saw me in the waiting room as he was leaving one night and asked me, why are you still here? Why don't you go home to sleep, he is in good hands? I said, I will be here until he comes home. I did not want to go into detail on why. I worked in hospitals, nursing homes, and private duty home health. I did not like how patients were treated in nursing when the patients' family was not around. There was a time when I was visiting Charles in ICU when his blood pressure was rising and I pressed the call button, the nurses were chatting away. I walked out to the nurse's station and told them what was going on and two nurses rushed into his room.

I went home after morning visiting hours to take shower and change clothes. Then we went back to the hospital for afternoon & evening visiting hours. After that, I stayed in the waiting room near ICU every night with my laptop, phone, warm blanket & warm clothes for 3-4 days. I rang the buzzer through the night to check on Charles. All the nurses knew who I was. The Lord kept him through it all and gave us 11 more years from that major heart attack in 2005. We were so grateful and made many memories.

We looked forward to vacation time with our granddaughters, taking rides to Galveston or weekend gateways and our Friday night dates and so much more. We took the girls to Galveston beach often and also took them to Moody Gardens for shows and the aquarium. After it was safe for Charles to travel again, we took our granddaughters on vacation annually.

In 2010 we went visited family in Hampton Georgia and went on to the Biltmore Estate in Asheville NC, Chimney Rock State Park in Chimney Rock, NC. It was difficult for Charles to walk on the trails and up to the mountain, he had to rest often, but he made it to the top. We found out there was an elevator that we could've taken to get to the top instead of walking the entire way. We were so disappointed that the waterfall was not that great flow like in the movie, "The last of the Mohican" waterfall scene, the fight scene and bathing scene was filmed at Chimney Rock State Park. The cabin where we stayed for nine days was in Lake Lure, NC. The movie "Dirty Dancing" was filmed in several areas in Lake Lure. The cast and production team stayed at the 1927 Lake Lure Inn and Spa. In 2012- We traveled to Panama City and Destin Florida, South Padre, Tx for horseback riding.

In 2015, we took our last vacation together with Caelan. Davian decided to stay home that year because she had a event to attend. Brae our youngest granddaughter at the time was 1 year old. We went to San Antonio, Austin, and The Island in Lago Vista TX & Burleson to visit my sister and her husband. We had planned to go to Salt Lake City, Utah. I found a nice 3-bedroom house with a nice backyard. It had great reviews about cleanliness, location, and the owners. Charles decided it was not the best time to take a long trip and I was ok with it. Later that year we decided to take our 3 granddaughters (Brae, Cae & Davian) to Palm Beach/Moody Gardens in Galveston, Texas. It was extremely hot that day, but the girls enjoyed being in the water. Brae loved the water! Davian & Cae played with her in the toddler pool for a while, then I told them to go enjoy the water where teens and adults were. I stayed with Brae in the toddler pool for a little while longer. Then Charles & I sat back at our picnic table with Brae watching Davian &

Caelan in the inner tube floats just relaxing and enjoying themselves. We loved seeing our babies have fun and just being kids. I always pack sandwiches, chips, fruit, water & juices. After they dried off and changed into their clothes, we took them to the Rainforest and the Aquarium.

I started going to pain management chiropractors to get hot and cold packs plus massages that would bring me some comfort when my pain level was up from stress at work. I would tell the medical assistant, please let the chiropractor know that my pain level is 10 and I'm sensitive to touch. I could hear her sharing my concerns with him as he approached her desk. This time I was almost in tears; I brought my recent MRI & CT-Scan. He asked me to come into his office as he looked at the CD, he said, Mrs. Comeaux, I'm not a specialist, but my gut tells me you have an autoimmune disease. The pain that you're describing has nothing to do with your back. He went on to say, "Your spine looks better than mine." He wanted to send me to a lab to do bloodwork, but my insurance wouldn't cover the order for him

After going to Charles Cardiologist in 2014, he did blood work and I tested positive for Lupus, RA, and connective tissue disease. Then in 2015, I was diagnosed with Lupus, RA, Sjogren's & Fibromyalgia by a Rheumatologist. At first, I went to the emergency room around the same time each year because of severe bone, muscle, joint & nerve pain. I was relieved but overwhelmed. Before that, I was seeing a Neurologist/Spine Care doctor who was relating all the pain to my back. I had a high pain tolerance and refused to take any kind of pain meds because I always felt nauseated and ended up vomiting most of the time, I could not hold it on my stomach. felt overwhelmed and wondered if I was cursed.

May 9, 2015- Charles, Kenneth (my brother) & I went to a jazz concert in Galveston, Texas where one of our favorite artists, Peter White, along with several others. It was a hot day, but later that evening it was a pleasant breeze. It was a day to remember. This was our second time going to a concert to see Peter White. Charles went up to him during intermission to talk to him. Peter was down-to-earth & patient while Charles shared how much he loved his music. Kenneth had mentioned that if we went to another Jazz concert that he would like to be included. Charles was always willing to drive an hour or so to pick up Kenneth because he knew I wanted to be there for him even more since Kenneth lost his vision in 2002. He had always been there for his siblings, and I wanted to be there for him to support him in any way I could plus we always had so much fun together. At one point, I would travel for American Council of the Blind annual conference to be there with Kenneth. He was the president of ACBT for six years, He worked hard and started a chapter where he lives in Beaumont. He has a faithful board that works with him, and they are helping many that are visually impaired. I am a member of that chapter and attend monthly meetings.

November 2015- Was the last time we celebrated Charles' birthday and Thanksgiving together which fell on the same day that year. He turned 74 and the oldest granddaughters switched his candles around to 47 to add some humor. Thanksgiving was at Charlotte & Jeffrey's this time. BraeLynn, our youngest granddaughter was one at this time. She sat on Papa's lap and every time he would talk to anyone but her, she would get his attention by calling him saying Papa several times. It was a memorable day.

In February 2016- BraeLynn was just turning two years old. We always had a separate birthday party with our granddaughters at our house along with ice cream and cake. We sang happy birthday to her, and she tried to read her card to us lol. Who knew this would be her last birthday with her grandpa. My oldest brother had a heart attack. The artery that was clogged was the one behind the heart like Charles experienced years before. A stent was placed in the heart and a few days later he was sent home. We went to Lake Charles, Louisiana to visit along with other family members. It turned out to be a big birthday gathering for him since his birthday is in February also. It was a lot of fun and laughter with family.

Saying Goodbye To A Significant Part of Our Lives

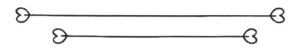

March 9, 2016- The weather report showed that it would be severe thunderstorms and heavy rainfall with flooding. Charles woke up earlier that day to keep an eye on the news for any updates on the weather for me. I woke up at my regular time around 4:15 am for prayer and to get ready for work but hoping that I would receive a text from work telling me that the office was closed for the day. Well, it was getting close to my time to leave and the weather in our area was not as bad as expected. I wanted to stay home that day.

It seemed like the severe weather waited until I got off. Charles and I spoke every day around noon and then after 5:00 pm when I was on my way home. This day was no different, we talked for about 20-25 minutes. We reminded each other that Friday was coming up (our date night) which we both looked forward to each week. We both said I love you at the end of the conversation as usual. Traffic was always worse in the rain. It took me over an hour to get home. I pressed the remote to open the garage. While it was opening, I expected to see Charles come out of the house to help me carry my rolling cart. I sat in the car for a few minutes, thinking he must be in the restroom. After a few minutes, there was no Charles. I became concerned and left everything in the car and rushed into the house. Charles was sitting on the couch with his head laid back as if he were sleeping. I called out to him, baby! baby! I said you are sleeping hard. Still, there was no response or movement.

I went closer to touch him, he was not cold but lukewarm, but he was not breathing. I called 911 and the operator instructed me to do CPR while I was waiting for the paramedics to arrive. Still nothing…The paramedics arrived and started to work on him while one of the guys ask questions. It was about 6 -7 guys working on him.

The young man that supervised the team, ask for Charles medication list. He said, ma'am, we have a live doctor that we consult with, we have everything that the emergency room has without the paperwork and the wait. I decided to call my aunt Edith to start a prayer call and then I called Charles's cardiologist to let him know what was going on. After several minutes of trying to resuscitate him. The young man in charge said ma'am, I am so sorry, we have done all we could. He said, "I can tell there was a lot of love in this home, you can see it in the family pictures. From that moment what I knew in my head was confirmed. Everything seemed so distant & far away like I was looking at someone else's life.

When the paramedics left a police force, officer arrived and asked to see Charles's meds and confirm the time of death. He asked who was coming to pick up the body. I told him my daughter and granddaughters were on their way. It took an hour for Charlotte and the girls to get there since they lived on the Northeast side of Houston and the traffic was worse than normal since it was raining hard.

The police officer told me to let Charlotte and the girls know they could not come and do all that screaming. I just looked at him and shook my head. I didn't realize there were rules on how you handle an unexpected loss. I sat at the dining table as I watched Charles's body lying on the living room floor for hours, from the time the paramedics left to the time the funeral home came to pick up the body. I was aware of what was happening in my mind, but my heart was in denial. Thoughts went through my mind like I cannot stay here tonight, I will go to a hotel. I watched Charlotte and my granddaughters say goodbye to daddy/grandpa. Charlotte called the funeral home that buried her firstborn (my grandson). She said, mom, you cannot stay here, you can come home with us. I said no I am tired; I will stay here. She insisted that one of the girls stay with me, Caelan volunteered. I did not sleep well. I cleaned up the living room and vacuumed before I went to bed, and I was in a lot of physical pain.

I felt sad for Brae, she did not understand how we celebrated her second birthday on February 8, 2016, and Charles died on March 9, 2016. She had finally got to the point after he started feeding her, where she loved being with her grandpa. When they would come over, He would call out her name with his loud voice and would say come, kiss papa! After his death, she would ask us when is Jesus sending grandpa back to us?

After The Loss

Early the next morning after Charles's death, I walked into the living room and saw his empty recliner, I looked outside in the backyard and in the garage to make sure that it was not all a bad dream. Reality started to kick in, he was gone. I sat down in my chair and sobbed, then I realized that I needed to call my job to speak to someone in human resources.

The person who I needed to speak to was not available, as I was leaving a voicemail message, I burst into a loud cry and woke up my granddaughter Caelan who decided to stay a couple of days with me. She ran into the living room with a box of Kleenex and said, grandma, are you okay? I apologized for being so loud as she comforted me. My phone kept ringing; I started to feel overwhelmed and asked her to answer all incoming calls. Once I realized I was no longer numb. The bandage was off, and the pain was severe.

My sister and niece wanted to visit, but I could not commit to anything the day of or the day after. I needed space, no questions, no demands, I did not want to talk to or see anyone for a few days. My daughters convinced me to allow my close friends to come to visit because they wanted to be there for me. I was so glad to see them. Kim, Bernadette & Zujeyn had proven to be genuine friends that God placed in my life. We all worked for the same company. This visit opened the door for more visits. My niece Dwana called and asked if she could visit and bring my aunt Edith, Barbara, my cousin & my friend Linda. I must admit It was comforting and fun. I remember in the early stages of grieving; I had a selfish thought. I would see people laughing and living life and I thought for a second, how could they? My husband is gone! It was like the whole world was on freeze, but it was only my world.

I woke up each morning and went into the living room, I said Lord, I am here! I sat in silence before the Lord for days before I was able to pray again. I was so broken, surely there was comfort & peace just sitting in His presence. Eventually, I started searching for scriptures to help me get through each day.

Psalm 147:3-He heals the brokenhearted and binds up their wounds.

Psalm 34:18- The Lord is close to the brokenhearted; he rescues those whose spirits are crushed.

Psalm 31:9- O' Lord, have mercy on me in my anguish. My eyes are red from weeping; my health is broken from sorrow. I put God in remembrance of His word, speaking these scriptures and many more…

I felt so lost, not knowing what to do. I started going to church with Charlotte and Jeffrey and my granddaughters, just to be with family. Shawn and Charlotte stay close to me, one on each side. When I felt like I was too weak to stand, they would lift me up. I had to keep in mind that they were grieving also. I remember going up for prayer, my daughters went up with me. Pastor Cannings prayed for me.

The Funeral & Final Goodbyes

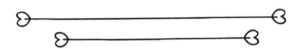

Once my daughter Shawn came in from California, we were able to set the funeral date for March 19, 2016. My youngest daughter Charlotte was a blessing working with the funeral home, on the obituary, gathering pictures for a presentation of Charles's life. The funeral was in Beaumont, Texas and we lived in Houston we had to make a couple of trips to the funeral home and the church. We were able to do most things by phone and email. I was surrounded by family and friends. Charles has 4 children from his first marriage, they were at the funeral and sat in the front row with us. Their children, some great grandchildren, his siblings and their children, his friends, nieces & nephews, neighbors traveled from

Houston, my family from different parts of Texas and Louisiana was there and my niece Ariana came from California, which meant the world to me.

I didn't want to do the repast thing, I just wanted to go back home. Charles's sister was doing a repast at her house. The thought of going there was very hard for me, I knew I would be crying wishing he was there. My Aunt Edna who was in her 80's at the time called me with her sweet soft voice and said, Deborah please let me do this for you. I couldn't say no to her. It was beautiful to spend time with Aunt Edna and Aunt Edith, my dad's last two sisters living. My daughters, granddaughters, nieces and a couple of my siblings and myself took pictures with them for memories.

Most of our neighbors, loved Charles. If they needed advice, someone to talk to or help with a project, they would call on him. One neighbor came by while Shawn was cleaning the garage and he asked where her dad was. When she told him that

Charles passed, he broke down crying, laying his head on her shoulder. It caught her off guard, she didn't know what to do. Also, about a month later one of the neighbors on the street behind us rang the doorbell, I said, who is it? He said his name and asked if my husband was home. I said, no my husband died over a month ago. I never opened the door but looked through the peephole and he was bent over crying.

One of the most challenging times was when I had to go grocery shopping after Charles's death. When I walked into the store, I felt overwhelmed, and my mind was flooded with memories of us going to the store together and when I would go alone to pick up his favorites. As I looked up and saw the soup aisle, I fought to hold the tears back. At that moment, I had to face the fact that I would not be purchasing these items anymore. I just wanted to fall on the floor and scream. I had to leave; it was too much too soon! I sat in my car crying out to the Lord asking him to help me.

It was so unbearable at times. I remember saying to the Lord, this is too painful, I do not want to go through this dark valley again. Lord, can you speed up the process? I heard him say, you must go through it so you can heal, I will not forsake you. At that moment, I pictured Him reaching out to me and I held His hand tightly. I knew if I suppress my emotions and did not deal with grief and pain like I did with Drew's death. Grief would show up in some form and most likely at an inopportune time.

Grief showed up in my life years later when I was married to Charles, and I had to deal with it then. You cannot run or hide from the pain of grief. Deal with it now so you do not have to later. I struggled when it was time to go back to work. I stayed home for almost 3 weeks, (2 wks. for bereavement & 1 wk. vacation). My supervisor called me to let me know that HR was pressing her for my return date. I was not ready to face people on the job because I did not want to answer any questions or reply to some of the most callous remarks. I knew I could have a breakdown at any time. The waves of grief could hit at any time. I would be laughing one minute and then crying the next. There were reminders of Charles everywhere.

He had done most of the cooking since he retired first. If I needed alterations or ironing done, he was the man, he did laundry, cleaned the house, did the yard work, fill-up & washed my car every weekend and so much more. I felt lost & incomplete. I always thought that I was an independent woman and sure of myself and what I wanted in life, but after Charles's death, I wondered who I was, apart from being Charles's wife? Was I experiencing an Identity crisis? Losing my husband meant losing a lifetime of shared experiences, conversations, and memories that were created for us to share only with each other. I missed us being grandparents together.

I loved the times Charles and I spent with our granddaughters. Whether it was for the weekend, holiday vacation, our yearly vacation getaway, or planning a picnic at the park or the beach when they were coming over for the weekend or holidays. I planned our time together as memorable events. I can't thank God enough for His total restoration of our marriage and family life. The latter was greater than the former years. When I think about today, I say, thank you, thank you Lord!!!!

I spent a lot of time with my daughters, granddaughters & my son-in-law after Charles death. On one of our trips to clean Charles's grave and put some flowers down, we went out to eat at one of our favorite seafood restaurants. We were reminiscing about some fun times we shared with Charles and laughing so much and a few minutes later we were crying uncontrollably. Once I stopped crying, I looked around and wondered if the server and the customers noticed the drastic shift in emotions at our table.

There were many times, I felt like I wanted to be around family and friends but when I was with them, I wanted to go home, I felt so disconnected. I did not feel like I belonged anywhere. I did not want to make any major decisions because I could not trust my emotions. One thing I was sure of was that I had to move. There were several reasons I needed to move. First, there were too many memories in the house, I could not bear it. Also, the drive to visit my daughters and granddaughters was at least an hour away. It even felt like my drive to and from work got longer. There was no motivation to drive home from work because there was nothing to look forward to but an empty house. Sometimes I would go out to eat with my friend Rebecca. I felt comfortable being with her and sharing what I was going through, even though she did not understand most of it, she listened and was always available to go to lunch or dinner.

I prayed to find a group of widows that could relate to what I was going through. All grief is not the same even though there are similarities. I found three griefshare groups near my area. I planned to visit all three to see where I would feel connected. The first group was the one. When these women started to share, exactly what I had been going through. There were mostly widows and 2 widowers. They understood the pain of losing a spouse. I needed to be in the company of women who had been married for years and now actually felt like half a person after the death of their husband. When I attended the first meeting, I listened to the women while they shared about their relationship and the pain of the loss. I burst into tears because they were describing exactly what I was feeling. It became a haven for me. I look forward to my weekly meetings.

The leader of the group took us out for dinner before the last meeting. I stayed in touch with 3 of the ladies for a while. I wanted to continue going to grief share once I moved, but it was no place/church near my new home. The couple of the meetings that I found were close to the end of the 8-week session. I wanted to make up the first two meetings since I came in on week three. I wished my church, and more churches would open the door for griefshare, but not put everyone in the same group.

I also went to a Christian therapist to whom my daughter referred me. She was genuinely nice, but grief counseling was not her specialty. I did love her format; she would begin the meeting with prayer and end the meeting with prayer. She would encourage me to take some quiet time afterward to hear God's voice.

In closing, she would pray for me, and then I would pray for her. She was surprised when I asked to pray for her. She said, none of her clients ever offered to pray for her before. I went there for a short while, 3 to 4 weeks.

There were days I was in so much physical pain in addition to the pain that comes with grief. Many nights I cried out to the Lord for relief. He heard me and answered me. In my brokenness & heartache, As I drew near to God, I experienced His presence and His unfailing love. I knew that my help would come from Him if I was going to make it out of this dark valley. I was so broken, I held on to Him for dear life. I realized it was ok to be vulnerable with God. Even though it was a difficult time, it was the most intimate time with God. When I look back, **there was beauty in my pain & brokenness,** but I could not see it then.

Lamentations 3:22-23 (NKJV)- Through the Lord's mercies, we are not consumed, because His compassions fail not. They are new every morning; Great is your faithfulness.

The Griefshare leader of my group gave us a book about Finding Comfort As You Journey Through Loss "Grieving With Hope" by Samuel J. Hodges, IV and Kathy Leonard. This book will bring some comfort from others that have experienced grief. Some of your questions will be answered and will also receive Godly counsel to help you through your grieving season.

Helpful Tips

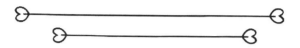

The most important thing to remember, is to move toward God not away from Him.

- Sit still before Him when you don't know how to pray.
- Talk to Him, express what you're feeling whether it be anger, despair, loneliness, or fear.
- He wants to hear from you, He loves you.
- Without His healing, you can't move forward, you will end up in a "stuck stage."
- Press through even when you want to give up, you'll be glad you did.
- Your surrender is required through grieving.

- Surrender to God what you can't handle and don't understand.
- Find a grief support group, connect with people who can relate to your pain.
- You may not want to go to every gathering or event and that's ok, but sometimes it's important just to get out of the house.
- If you draw closer to God, He will draw close to you.
- He will never forsake you or leave you, even when don't feel like He's there.
- The holidays was the hardest, I pressed forward for my daughters and granddaughters.

Life After

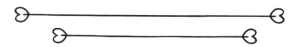

I knew I had to decide what to do about Charles belongings, I didn't want to just hold on to things just to say I had them, plus I was downsizing and didn't have the extra room in my new place. Certain items the girls wanted; his guitar that I bought him for one of his birthday gifts, he self-taught himself through videos and just listening to his favorite jazz songs by Peter White. I gave that to Shawn because she had Drew's guitar also. She said I have both of my dad's guitars. Shawn came to help me pack. She packed Charles closet because she was trying to spare me. I could hear her crying as she packed his things. We found a Veteran's charity that accepted all his clothes and shoes. Shawn put it in her car and took it to the place later.

The outpouring of support from family & friends with calls, texts, cards & visits meant a lot to me once I let people in. At first, I didn't want to be overwhelmed with visitors and advice telling me how to grieve or what to expect. I needed time to think, accept and embrace being a widow, Yes, I said embrace. Allowing the grief to run its course, acknowledging that I was angry, sad, brokenhearted, lost, lonely and all emotions that rose up in me during this time. God knew what I was feeling, and He was the only one that could help me through this. Staying open and honest with Him activated the healing process.

In October 2016, seven months after Charles death. My oldest sister died from ovarian cancer. Ella, Kenneth, and I had been praying about going to California to visit Anna while she was still alive. We also wanted to be there to support our niece Ariana at the time, but it didn't work out for us to get there in time. We ended up traveling to be there for the memorial services. During my review, my supervisor reminded me that I had no vacation time left. But God gave me favor and I was given 5 bereavement days since this was the death of my sister. I took additional days without pay. It was a special time for our family. It had been a while since the five youngest children were all together at one time. There were tears, hugs and so much laughter. It was nice to see my nephews and nieces I hadn't seen in a long time and to have lunch with my friend Ursula. When we returned to Houston, God did some unexpected work with and in us. There was some healing needed in my relationship with my sister Ella. God opened the door for us to talk about it thoroughly.

Throughout the years, I've noticed God's unconditional love whenever there's been a death in my family, someone was pregnant and within a few months we are celebrating a new life. Which has brought so much joy, hope, and comfort to all who were grieving.

November 2016 was Charles' birthday month and Thanksgiving; it was very emotional but the blessing and highlight of the month was that my youngest granddaughter (Sydney) was born on November 14, 2016. Charlotte named her Sydney because on Charles original birth certificate his name was Sidney. Neither of his sisters knew about this. We found out when we went to the courthouse to get a copy of his birth certificate. He had to change it to Charles. There were a lot of misspelled errors back in the day. Charles was older than me so it's a possibility that he was delivered by a midwife. My aunt told me that her son and I were born in the hospital basement like many black babies in Louisiana in the 50's. This occurred in Louisiana and some other southern states. The only birth certificate I had that I found in one of my mom's old purses after she died was from St

Patrick's Hospital with my footprints and her thumbprints on the back of the document. Charles and I made special trips to the courthouses in Beaumont and Lake Charles because I just wanted to have copies just in case, we needed them later. I found out my full name was not on my birth certificate either. When I told the clerk my name, she typed it in and said we don't have anything with Deborah Semien in our records. My mind started to wander, then she asked, what is your middle name? When I told her it came right up "Elaine Semien" Charles, and I couldn't believe what we had just learned. I had to send in a check and completed paperwork to New Orleans to add my first name to my birth certificate. My daughter Charlotte joked about how she thought her parents were Charles and Deborah all these years, but it was Sidney & Elaine.

January 2017, I had an outpatient procedure done. My siblings (Ella & Carl) came to visit for a few days. They cooked and helped in any way they could as I recovered. I really didn't want to go back to work, and my family questioned why but I knew it was not time to stop yet. It became harder to walk from the garage to the office and at the end of the day to walk back to the car. The physical pain of forcing my body to go further each day became overbearing. I heard the Lord say, I will honor your faith. I understood that to mean I would have to trust Him as my provider. I had been praying and asking God when I could retire. I heard Him say, **in** due season. I said Lord, what does that mean? Of course, the scripture **Galatians 6:9** came to mind.

I needed a clearer understanding of what God was saying and I did get it. God was saying in **His timing** (not mine). Of course, I had a different idea on what my retirement would look like. I was hoping to get an early retirement package. That was not God's plan. God was doing a work in me. My Rheumatologist filled out medical forms stating my limitations and restrictions for lifting, bending &

stooping. These forms had to be filled out every three months and faxed to HR.

On February 27, 2017- I woke up and could barely walk. This was a bad flare. I pressed on because I knew I had to be in a quarterly meeting. It was my supervisor, myself, HR Director & an HR assistant who I met with every three months. I was told by the HR Director that they could no longer accommodate me by following the doctor's restrictions. She told me to ask the doctor what she would like them to do at this point.

I could not believe what I was hearing. Was she going to ignore the doctor's order? I called my Rheumatologist when I got back to my desk and asked if she could see me the next day. On February 28, 2017- I went in that morning to talk to my doctor, she was shocked that an HR person said that. She encouraged me to go on disability and she would fill out the paperwork. I called the HR director and told her I would not be returning to work because of the doctor's orders. This was my second Rheumatologist

Meanwhile, I continue planning an Autoimmune Awareness luncheon that I had started working on in the latter months of 2016. The event was scheduled for March 13, 2017, because March was Autoimmune Awareness month. This was to educate and bring awareness by sharing my story, my daughter Shawn shared her journey with Fibromyalgia and couldn't walk for 7 years, also Crystal (my niece by marriage) shared the story of her mom having MS. We also had a guest speaker that educated us on type 1 diabetes that is an organ-specific autoimmune disease caused by the autoimmune response against pancreatic B cells. The speaker also spoke a little about Type 2 diabetics (not considered to be an autoimmune disease) she shared healthy meals recipes. My friend Kim made t-shirts for everyone that volunteered that day. She had her table set up with items that she made. My supporters and volunteers included my daughters, granddaughters, my brother Kenneth, and my sister Ella.

It was a long year filled with a lot of paperwork to apply for my long-term disability through MetLife and they managed filing for my Social Security Disability. Harvey hit Houston in that year, so my Long-Term Disability Insurance did not get to the New York office until August 2017. I received a paycheck every other week until all sick pay & vacation was paid. When I thought it was over, there were a few more checks that came through. God provided all my needs in so many ways. I was glad to be home where I was able to grieve freely and not be under additional stress from the job.

2017 was the first for a lot of things. I stayed connected to family, friends, and other believers for support. There were days when I felt sad, miss him terribly. Certain things I just wanted to share with him and no one else. I still cried when I heard our favorite songs, his birthday in November and the holidays were difficult. I pressed through for my granddaughters because God only knows how hard it was for them. It brought joy to our family when Sydney (my youngest granddaughter) was born on November 14, 2017. God knew this little girl would help us to heal. She favored Charles and we start to notice his sense of humor at an early age. I remember the first time I kept her for Charlotte and Jeffrey. I cried when I realized she would never get to experience his love and I would not be able to share this joy with him as I did with our other granddaughters.

In 2017, Shawn, Charlotte & I went to our first Inspire Women's Conference. It was such a beautiful experience. Six years later I'm still connected to Inspire Women. God has used this ministry to bless me and has connected me to some admirable women of God, some powerful prayer partners and other widows through this ministry.

Charlotte and I enrolled in the Inspire Women Leadership Academy and graduated in 2018. It's a one-year accredited signature course that offers practical content-based teachings on God's Word to help you overcome loneliness, rejection and fear to finish well. It helps you find clarity by matching your God-given passion to your purpose for God. You learn how to transform your emotions of loneliness, rejection, and fear into power to finish your mission for God.

In March 2019, my brother Jimmy died and in November 2019-My brother Nolan died Ella and I went to California for Nolan's memorial services and to support his children and grandkids. We stayed with our niece in Long Beach. We were able spend time with nieces and nephews we hadn't seen in years. The best part of the trip was that I got a chance to go to the beach and the weather was in the

70's. I love California beaches and weather. Unfortunately, Ella came down with a respiratory infection, so we thought. She had a fever and was coughing a lot. No confirmation of what she had. There were reported cases of COVID-19 in December 2019 in Wuhan China.

The World Health Organization declared COVID-19 a pandemic on March 11, 2020. Life as we knew it, changed drastically. I didn't see my daughters or grandchildren much during this time, I wanted us all to stay safe, I missed them so much. Charlotte would come by the cast iron fence that surrounded my apartment complex and I could talk to the kids. We had a virtual Thanksgiving and Christmas. I made the cornbread dressing, Charlotte and Davian did the rest. They came by to drop my plate off by the fence and I gave them a portion of the dressing. At the time, we lived close to each other.

In January 2021, The number of cases in the U.S. decreased, but more variants were spreading. Wisdom was a necessity during those times, not just being foolish and going whenever and wherever. May 2021 the and a virtual Mother's Day tea party with my two daughters and my four granddaughters. Meeting virtually either Facebook or Zoom became popular and necessary for me to stay connected, not only with my family but with my church group, Inspire Women Ministry monthly prayer group and Inner Circles group. I was so emotional at every inner circle meeting during the pandemic. I shared a lot about being a widow and the loss I experienced. One day as Anita and I was texting, she said, I'm gonna pray that God heals your heart, I can't explain how much those words blessed me. Even though His word says, he heals the broken hearted and binds their wounds. I had been speaking Ps 147: 3 over my life from the beginning. Today, seven years later, I believe my heart is healed. During the pandemic I missed hugging my family, friends, and my Inspire Women sisters. My prayer life increased because so many people I knew were losing loved ones. I started ordering groceries online way before the pandemic, so I continued doing that and went to pick them up or have them delivered. I felt a strong conviction to witness and share God's goodness during this time because no one knew what each day would bring.

I went through some lonely days and missed Charles a lot during that time. It comforted me to pray for others. I had to remind myself that we were in a pandemic and things were not normal as we knew it. It was such a sadness and uncertainty hanging over us. I had to stay connected with God in prayer, so that depression would not creep in. Times like this made me more grateful to know Jesus as my Lord and Saviour. I was so glad when I could finally spend time with my granddaughters and get together with family again.

In September 2021 Anita, the founder of Inspire Women asked if I could attend the conference and afterwards make calls to those who attended, to get their comments about the conference and asking them if they needed prayer. This was so rewarding. I trusted God's to lead me how to pray for each person's need. God moved in people's lives and in mine, it was a two-fold blessing. This project was approximately 2 months. I continued making calls for Inspire Women and praying with several women, God connected me to some powerful prayer partners and some widows who I still pray for today.

In December 2021 Kenneth and I traveled to Crowley, Texas to visit our sister Ella. She had a stroke in November 2021. We hoped that she would be home so we could spend Christmas with her in her home, but She was still in a rehab facility when we arrived. We made the best of our visit by spending time with her each day. We also enjoyed our time with our brother Carl. We brought Ella home cooked meals daily. I prepared a hearty Christmas meal for the family and brought Ella a plate. She was so grateful and glad to see her siblings, her husband, daughter, son in law, granddaughter, and great grandson.

In June 2022, while visiting Living Word Fellowship with my daughter and her family as I did at least once a month. There was an announcement about tuition free classes offered to those who were interested. The founders started OBA in 2015 and were graduates of Dallas Theological Seminary. They thought it would be good to share what they've learned with others for free. This was good to hear. I looked over at my daughter and her husband thinking this would be good for them, but I felt the nudge in my spirit, I knew it was for my ears because it was something I desired but every time I saw a program with a deeper study in the bible, It was always more than I could afford.

I attended the orientation class to hear more about the academy and felt pressed to enrolled in The Opened Bible Academy in June. I started class on July 26, 2022. The professors that teach the classes are phenomenal. It is a two-and one-half year course and then there will be a graduation ceremony. The professors challenge us in creative thinking which heightens my knowledge in God's word as God gives me understanding. I am so grateful for this opportunity. Each day is a new adventure with God.

Every day is a walk of faith, I make plans, but God orders my steps. Drama, mess, and pettiness have no place in my life. I try to take advantage of every opportunity to share the good news of the gospel which is, Jesus Christ died on the cross for our sins and rose from the dead. Having health challenges and limitations has actually helped me to rely on God even more and wait on Him instead of getting in His way. When God opens a door, I walk through it.

It's been seven years since Charles transitioned. I believe this is my year of completion for that chapter of my life. My heart is no longer broken, God has healed my broken heart. My relationship with my Saviour is no longer just head knowledge it is now heart knowledge. I'm excited about this new season even though I don't know what it all entails. My trust is in God. He has been so faithful!

I moved near my daughters when Charles died. My sister and I prayed for God's will when it would be time to move again. I knew this was temporary. First Shawn moved a year or so after I moved. It was okay because my granddaughters were just 2 minutes away. I was ready to move to a Senior community. From 2017-2022, I started adding my name on several waiting lists. No matter how bad I wanted to move, I wasn't going ahead of

God. Every year before my lease renewal I would talk to the Lord to see if this would be the year. One time I said Lord, my deadline is up on June 1st. The Lord said, that's your deadline.

Things start to shift after Davian (my oldest granddaughter) graduated. She met the man she was going to marry. They were married in February 2022.

In 2022 Charlotte and her family moved to a different area 45 minutes to an hour away from me. It's something that we prayed for, and this was God's timing. I had gotten used to them being so close if I needed them or they needed me. I was happy for them because they needed a bigger home and a safer and healthy environment for the kids to thrive in. This was God's timing for them. I helped them unpack when they moved and for at least the first 3 months, I spent a week there. It was like a getaway for me, and the drive was too long to go for a day. Meanwhile, my studies, prayer partners that

God placed in life, ministry with widows and women with autoimmune issues kept me busy. Still being connected to Inspire Women was an added blessing. My life was full.

I've always had a difficult time with changes. I once viewed changes as something bad. Because God is Lord of my life, I now embrace changes.

In June 2023 marked seven years that I was living at the apartment complex since Charles died. Seven symbolizes completion. I reflected on the years passed and realized that I made it through my grieving season and my heart was no longer broken. When I think of Charles, I smile. I will always be grateful for the work God did in us, in our marriage, the restoration of our family and the additional 11 years that God gave us from 2005 to 2016 when it seemed like it was the end when his heart stopped. God has been so faithful! Through all my trials and suffering when the enemy tried to break me and make me turn my back on God. I continued to cry out to Him and He heard me and answered me each time.

Ps. 46:1- **God** is our refuge and strength, a very present help in trouble.

This devotional from Crosswalk resonated with me.

Nothing before Its Time By Clarence L. Haynes Jr.

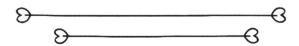

There is so much more I want to tell you, but you can't bear it now." - John 16:12 (NLT)

I want to share with you a truth that I have learned about myself. I often desire immediate answers, quick progress, and instant blessings (don't look at me funny, you probably do the same thing). Yet, over the years, I have realized God operates in my life with order, process, timing, and progress.

Today, I invite you to join me in exploring the beauty of God's perfect timing and his intentional process in your life. God's process with you is intentional. As a believer in Jesus, there is one thing you must come to grips with. There are no accidents or coincidences in God's plan for your life.

God is meticulous in his work in your life, and he does not overlook any detail. This is also true of what he allows in your life. Just as Jesus withheld information from his disciples until they were ready, our father does the same thing. God lovingly prepares you for each step in your journey and gives you nothing before it's time. There may be times when he withholds certain answers, trials, promotions, or blessings until you are ready to handle them. I know we can get impatient when he withholds blessings until we are ready, but he also does the same with trials. This is a testament to His love and mercy, as he not only knows what is best for your growth and well-being, but he knows when it is best for you as well.

If you are trusting God and His plan for your life, you are in good hands!

The Broken-hearted Widow

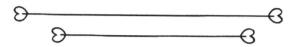

There were once two that became one flesh.

Now there's only one,

Walking through this dark valley, hoping to see the light.

Should I wait or shall my soul take flight?

Functioning with half a heart, and fewer beats than before.

Not knowing what's ahead, Oh Lord! There has to be more.

How can I bear this pain of a torn heart?

Please heal me and give me a fresh start.

You're the only One that can.

Your word says that you heal the brokenhearted and bind up their wounds.

Please lead and guide with your mighty hand.

Deborah Comeaux

Made in the USA
Monee, IL
05 February 2024

52452744R00103